CHRISTY BROWN

For my family and friends: Ann, Willy, Kelvin, Seán, Katriona, Eamonn, Kay, Paddy, Betty, Francy and my mother and father, without whom it would have been impossible to write this book.

CHRISTY BROWN

The Life that Inspired *My Left Foot*

Georgina Louise Hambleton

MAINSTREAM
PUBLISHING

EDINBURGH AND LONDON

First published in Great Britain in 2007 by
MAINSTREAM PUBLISHING COMPANY (EDINBURGH) LTD
7 Albany Street
Edinburgh EH1 3UG

ISBN 9781845962807

Extracts from *My Left Foot, A Shadow on Summer,
Wild Grow the Lilies, Down All the Days* and *Collected Poems* by
Christy Brown, published by Secker & Warburg, reprinted by
permission of The Random House Group Ltd

'Who's Who' by W.H. Auden, from *Collected Shorter Poems 1927–1957*,
reproduced by permission of Faber & Faber Ltd

The author has made every effort to clear all copyright permissions,
but where this has not been possible and amendments are required,
the publisher will be pleased to make any necessary
arrangements at the earliest opportunity

A catalogue record for this book is available
from the British Library

Typeset in Optima and Sabon

Printed in Great Britain by
Clays Ltd, St Ives plc

We need confidence and friendliness as well as, if not more than, medical treatment. It is not only our muscles and limbs which bother us – sometimes it is our minds as well, our inner selves that require more attention than our twisted arms and legs. A child with a crooked mouth and twisted hands can very quickly and easily develop a set of very crooked and twisted attitudes both towards himself and life in general, especially if he is allowed to grow up with them without being helped to an understanding of them. If the idea of his 'difference' as compared to normal children is allowed to take root in his mind, it will grow with him into adolescence and eventually into manhood, so that he will look out on life with a mind as distorted as his body. Life becomes to him just a reflection of his 'crookedness', his own emotional pain.

Christy Brown, *My Left Foot*

As for the exposure and rearing of children, let there be a law that no deformed child shall live.

Aristotle, *Politics*

Who's Who

A shilling life will give you all the facts:
How Father beat him, how he ran away,
What were the struggles of his youth, what acts
Made him the greatest figure of his day:
Of how he fought, fished, hunted, worked all night,
Though giddy, climbed new mountains; named a sea:
Some of the last researchers even write
Love made him weep his pints like you and me.

With all his honours on, he sighed for one
Who, say astonished critics, lived at home;
Did little jobs about the house with skill
And nothing else; could whistle; would sit still
Or potter round the garden; answered some
Of his long marvellous letters but kept none.

W.H. Auden

ACKNOWLEDGEMENTS

Thanks are due to the following artists, editors, agents, librarians, journalists and others: Victoria Belfrage, Didier Bidou, Cathy Boyle, Michael Breathnach, Anne Buckley, Bill Campbell, Michael Chen, Shane Connaughton, Professor Lennard J. Davis, Patricia Day, Daniel Day-Lewis, Tom Desmond, Gerard Dockery, Anna Doherty, Professor Terry Dolan, Ronnie Drew, Stijn Dulemare, Victoria Enright, Ciara Gibbons, Brian Hand, Seamus Heaney, Anthony Jordan, Neil Jordan, Claire Keegan, Brendan Kennelly, Eva Kopriosek, Gene Lambert, James Liddy, Brian Lynch, Alicia Macauley, Maura Mahon, Pat McBride, Maria McCudden, Geoff Mulligan, Dominic Murtagh, Bill O'Donnell, Sunniva O'Flynn, Emer Ryan, Sol Stein and Dicky Uthaman (and his family and staff).

I am grateful for time spent at the Irish Film Institute; the Irish College in Paris; the National Library of Ireland; Kirby's Pub in Ballyheigue, County Kerry; Link Internet store and call centre; Kilmainham Gaol; Marino Library; and Shakespeare and Company bookstore. Thanks to Bernard, Charlie and Olivia at TPS for their invaluable work.

My particular thanks to my family, John Banville, Adrian Dunbar, Eddie Holt, Professor Declan Kiberd, Loretta Longden, Professor Frank McGuinness, Dr Emilie Morin, Ulick O'Connor, Noel Pearson, Ariana Roseman, Peter Sheridan, Eoghan Smith and Jonathan Williams for their invaluable advice, close readings and support. And thank you to mo chú for being my very best friend.

CONTENTS

Chapter One
A BEGINNING *11*

Chapter Two
A MOTHER *17*

Chapter Three
A LETTER *31*

Chapter Four
A FRIENDSHIP *41*

Chapter Five
A DIAGNOSIS *53*

Chapter Six
A BOOK *69*

Chapter Seven
A LOVE AFFAIR *93*

Chapter Eight
A WRITER *103*

Chapter Nine
AN ARTIST *123*

Chapter Ten
AN INTERNATIONAL BESTSELLER *143*

Chapter Eleven
A WEDDING *161*

Chapter Twelve
A FUNERAL *181*

Chapter Thirteen
A FILM *197*

Chapter Fourteen
AN OSCAR *211*

Chapter Fifteen
AN ENDING *221*

SELECT BIBLIOGRAPHY
AND SOURCES *225*

INDEX *231*

Chapter One

A BEGINNING

I was born in 1932, in Dublin, the son of a brick-layer and the twelfth in a line of twenty-two, of which thirteen survived . . . I was born with a complaint called cerebral palsy resulting from injury to part of my brain that controls and coordinates movement. This left me completely paralysed except for the use of one limb – my left foot, with which I learned to draw, paint, write and nearly everything one normally does with one's hands. I never attended school and picked up my few scraps of knowledge from watching brothers and sisters with their homework, observing other people, and later on from books borrowed, stolen and occasionally bought in second-hand places on the quays.

Until the age of seventeen I could not talk except by my eyes and foot and a queer sort of grunting language understood only by my family. I attended a clinic later on in Dublin for some years, but was by that time too old to gain any lasting benefit from the treatment involved. In 1954 I wrote my life story, which was published in the same year in England and in America, and has since been translated into French, German, Italian, Dutch, Japanese and Braille . . . I hope someday to be a poet and put out a little volume of verse.

Christy Brown, writing to Liam Miller
of the Dolmen Press in Dublin,
1963

In 2003, I was an undergraduate literature student at University College Dublin and I had never heard of the artist and writer Christy Brown. I studied like crazy for the final exams for my degree course that year. My approach was lots of studying combined with taking taxis back and forth from college while living on copious cigarettes and endless cups of black coffee. One day, I took a taxi from the university back to my flat on the south side of Dublin city. While I was in the cab, the driver started to quiz me about the book I was reading, which happened to be *Ulysses*. There aren't many cities in the world where *Ulysses* would be a normal topic of conversation in a cab.

'What's that book about?' he asked me.

'Well, actually, I've only read a few chapters but apparently Joyce – you know, the guy who wrote it – well, from what I understand, he's rewriting the English language. It's mad and some of it I can't even read but parts of it are hilarious too . . .'

'Well, you know, he's the one Irish writer I could never read. I love to read. Have you ever read Behan?' he asked me.

'No,' I said. 'Do you mind if I smoke?'

'No bother, work away,' he told me. We chatted about books as we drove along and eventually he pulled up outside my house and lit a cigarette. He offered me another one. I accepted.

'Brendan Behan. Now, there's someone you should read. Brendan was hilarious. I knew him. You know the joke about Behan on his deathbed?'

'Nope, never heard it.'

'Well, Brendan was on his deathbed and, you know, he was famous for being a bit of a bastard – excuse my language, here, but he was. He hated the Catholic Church, Ireland, the English, everybody. He took the piss out of everyone. So, on his deathbed, he was surrounded by nuns, who all wanted him to accept the last rites, you know, the way loads of Catholics accept God right at the end.

'So these nuns were gathered around Brendan and they are

dying for him to take God into his life. And he was really ill, you know. Brendan was a heavy drinker. He got very sick in the end. So the nuns were wiping his brow and waiting, just waiting. Suddenly, Brendan called over one of the nuns.

'"Sister, sister, come here," he says.

'"Ah, what is it, Brendan? Are you all right?"

'"Lean close in to me, sister."

'She leaned in.

'"Closer," he says.

'She leaned in closer.

'"Sister," he whispered in her ear, "I hope all your sons grow up to be bishops."'

It took me a second to get it but then the penny dropped and I laughed.

'Brendan knew Christy Brown, you know.'

'Who?'

'The writer Christy Brown.'

'I can't say I have ever heard the name before,' I told him honestly.

'Ah, you do know him. They made his life into this great film called *My Left Foot*. That guy, what's-his-name, he won the Oscar for it. Christy was crippled, born into a huge family. He wrote with his left foot. He was a painter, too, and a great poet . . .'

'Oh yeah, I remember that movie,' I replied.

And, of course, I did. Everyone remembers the film *My Left Foot* because of the extraordinary performance for which 'that guy' – Daniel Day-Lewis – won an Oscar. But I didn't know anything about the writer Christy Brown, even though I had almost completed a pure English Literature degree at University College. In fact, the only reason I knew his name was because I had seen the film. I told the taxi driver as much.

'Well, he was a grand poet, a truly great writer. If you love books and Irish writers, you should go and find his family. They live just near here and they are so proud of him and his work.'

'Thanks, I will,' I told him, thinking I had no intention of doing any such thing. 'And thanks for the smokes, and the chat – that's one of the reasons I love living in Dublin.'

He smiled and drove off. I wrote down what the taxi driver had said in one of my journals but didn't think much more about it.

A year later, I was in serious need of a topic to write about for the Masters course in Anglo-Irish Literature and Drama I was doing at the same university. I hadn't expected to get on the course and so had not prepared anything for my thesis (a twenty-thousand-word, critical, academic piece of writing focusing on one Irish author), which made up a large part of the final mark for the year. So I decided to follow this crazy lead I had about this writer and painter no one had ever heard of called Christy Brown. Throughout an entire degree course in literature, from 1999 to 2003, I had never heard his name mentioned by the teachers I'd had, nor had I seen his work in any of the anthologies of Irish writing that I had often combed through on late nights to help me pass my exams.

I went to Kimmage, the part of Dublin the taxi driver had told me Christy Brown was from, and then to a local pub. After visiting the pub a few times (and on an average trip drinking more than a few pints of Guinness), I finally found someone who assured me that he knew Christy's brother Eamonn and he said that he would put me in touch with him (in fact, the guy turned out to have been the right-hand man to the famous Dublin criminal Martin 'The General' Cahill).

I then had to look at Christy Brown's writing. It turned out that the taxi driver was right: the man was a great poet. He had also written a novel, *Down All the Days*, that was as well received as any writer, publishing house or agent could hope for. In 1970, the book made Christy Brown a small fortune. Not only was his work exciting to me but his life story was unbelievable.

Christy was the twelfth child of twenty-two, of whom only

thirteen survived. During his birth, he was deprived of oxygen and as a result he suffered from double athetoid cerebral palsy for the rest of his life. The only part of his body he could control was his left foot. He shook constantly and could not walk, nor could he speak coherently. His disability meant he could never take himself to the toilet and he could never eat or drink when he wanted to (he had to be fed by someone else). Yet, with all this astonishing adversity that he faced in his life, it was not these challenges that inspired or amazed me; it was the words and imagery he used in his work and how unusually and beautifully he crafted them. I was fascinated by his work and although I was enthralled by his life story, I did not want to use his life as the basis for the academic piece of writing required for the course I was on (in fact, I believed at the time that biography was a very poor form of criticism). Instead, I wanted to find out all I could about his writing and why I had never seen or heard of it before.

I approached the then head of the English Department in which I studied, Professor Declan Kiberd, to ask him whether or not I could use Christy Brown as a subject and to find out what sources existed that looked at his novels, paintings and poetry in depth. He told me that yes, of course I could study Christy but no sources existed for the purposes of researching him. In fact, no one had looked in detail at his work, no biography had been written about him and no academic papers or journals discussed his art or literature. I was baffled by this but decided it would be a great experience and that I should go ahead anyway, and so I attempted to write a thesis on Christy Brown. Two years later, I was out of college and had two Masters degrees in literature and no job. So, I decided to write this book.

I read and reread Christy's work, talked for hours with his family and searched through his private papers (then undocumented and unread). I remember one night looking at some papers his brother had lent to me for research purposes.

As I opened the letters, not knowing what to expect, I noticed that the envelope I was holding in my hand bent slightly to one side, to the right. I realised this was because the last person to put the letter back in its envelope had been Christy, using his left foot – and that the envelope had probably not been opened for over thirty years. What was even more shocking was seeing the hundreds of letters he had typed with his toes. Each was dated, with the type angled slightly to the right; the letters contained pieces of prose which often made me weep or laugh out loud. There is only one letter I have found written by Christy Brown which contains any spelling errors. Reading those letters, I felt Christy was whispering to me over my shoulder and I listened intently, trying to discover who he was.

As his life had never been written before, I thought it a good idea to speak both with his family and with artists who knew or worked with him. Each interview referred to in this book was conducted by me (unless otherwise specified) for the sole purpose of trying to put Christy's life into the most accurate context I could. Words and phrases that most often came up when Christy was discussed were 'genius', 'a serious drinker', 'a survivor', 'great to be with', 'brave' and 'hilarious'. To tell Christy's story and to recount his life, I believe the best authorial voices are his own and those of his close family and friends, whose words follow, recounting a Dublin that is now very much forgotten and should be remembered. The members of Christy Brown's family who are still alive have stories that no one else could tell and they have agreed to tell them here. Thankfully, they all have in their possession an amazing power for storytelling, just as their brother did. It has been my privilege to write the life of such an extraordinary human being.

Chapter Two

A MOTHER

For a time – for a long and frightening time – I thought my mother's death had broken me completely in spirit as well as in body. The world held nothing for me. It was a jungle. I didn't want to live. Basically being a coward, I took the easy way out and drank to excess, substituting a false kind of death for the real thing. The more I drank the more hateful life seemed to me and the more hateful I seemed to become to myself . . . Instead of deadening my senses, the alcohol merely sharpened them and made me see myself as I really was – a blinded sort of animal wallowing in self-pity; I realised with some horror and some disgust that what I was grieving was not so much the loss of my mother, but the loss of her to me.

The sorrow was self-centred; I was not so much concerned about her probable welfare in the hereafter as about my own lost little self here on earth. I was like a child crying in the dark, shut up in my own tight little shell, bruised and battered and hating the world for the terrible thing it had done to me. I wasn't doing my mother much credit.

I was doing her a grave dishonour . . . I was throwing in the towel and wherever she is, she must have looked down on me with intense anger and displeasure. I was being untrue to her. I wasn't even being true to myself. She had given me something of her life, something of herself . . . she expected me to use it carefully . . . as a torch lighting up the dark places of my mind. Instead, I was drowning that precious part of her in me by drink, by self-pity, by deliberate idleness and indifference. I was desecrating the marvellous strength of her life and the great calm and dignity of her death. I was being a proper bastard. I still don't know where I am going.

Christy Brown, writing to his brother Seán,
30 November 1968,
two months after the death of their mother, Bridget Brown

In 1990, a small, low-budget Irish film entitled *My Left Foot* found tremendous success on the night of the Oscars. Its cast and crew had hoped simply that the film might do well in Ireland; instead, it was nominated for five Academy Awards: best picture (producer Noel Pearson), best director (Jim Sheridan), best actor in a leading role (Daniel Day-Lewis), best screenplay based on material from another medium (Jim Sheridan and Shane Connaughton) and best actress in a supporting role (Brenda Fricker). On 26 March, at the 62nd Annual Academy Awards Ceremony in Los Angeles, Brenda Fricker accepted the Oscar for best supporting actress for her role as Bridget Brown in *My Left Foot*. As the American actor Kevin Kline read out her name, Brenda gasped and mouthed, 'I don't believe it.' In her acceptance speech, she thanked Christy Brown, then almost ten years dead, 'just for being alive', and his mother, Bridget, because, as Fricker told the press afterwards, 'Any woman who gives birth to twenty-two children deserves one of these.'

Bridget Brown, née Fagan, was born on the north side of Dublin on 24 September 1901. The history of her biological parents is unknown. All her surviving family know of her early childhood is that she lived in a tenement house in Dublin. Conditions in the city's tenement housing were horrific and on 2 September 1913, two buildings collapsed in Church Street in the city centre. They had housed more than forty people, including Bridget Fagan's family; city authorities had inspected the buildings and declared them safe only a few weeks before. Many were injured and seven people were killed when the tenements collapsed. Bridget's parents and all her siblings died. She was left orphaned at the age of twelve. An inquiry set up after the incident discovered that 87,305 people lived in similar tenements throughout the city and most families had only one room.

After the disaster, Bridget's Uncle Kit, who lived in the Smithfield Market area, just north of the River Liffey, took her into his family. Uncle Kit and his family owned several pigs, which gave them a certain status in the community. Bridget remained in her new home until, at the age of sixteen, she met her future husband, Patrick Brown. Also aged sixteen when they met, Patrick lived in Old North King Street, which ran adjacent to the market area of Smithfield. He had served as a runner for the Irish Republican Brotherhood in his early teens and had been involved in the 1916 Rising; following the surrender of the insurgents, he had been interned in Kilmainham Gaol for a few days. After a year's courtship, Patrick proposed marriage. Bridget's family declared their disapproval of the union. Believing Patrick and his family to be below their station, they issued Bridget with an ultimatum: forget him or forget us. She chose to begin a new life with Patrick and they married in 1918. In her life, Bridget gave birth to fifteen sons and seven daughters; of those twenty-two, only thirteen survived past infancy: Liz, Tony, Jim, Mona, Paddy, Christy, Peter, Peggy, Eamonn, Seán, Francis, Ann and Danny.

For six years, the couple shared just two rooms in a five-storey tenement house in Dublin, where their first four children were born. The Church Street disaster that had orphaned Bridget had caused uproar in the Dublin papers, and the Irish government came under intense pressure to deal with the housing crisis in the city. From 1914 onwards, inner-city Dubliners were slowly moved out of their homes into new public housing on the western outskirts of the city. In the summer of 1924, Bridget, Patrick and their children packed up their belongings and set off on Patrick's brother's horse and cart to travel out to the area Dubliners called 'the dark lanes'. Today, Kimmage is part of Dublin's sprawling suburbs but in the early part of the twentieth century it was considered to be the wilds of the countryside. The families who were moved out of the city centre into the new corporation houses in Kimmage felt dislocated and isolated; it was as though they had been moved to the middle of nowhere. As Bridget's third son, Paddy, remembers: 'You moved into your corporation house and coming through the housing scheme, when you hit Sundrive Road, there were no shops, no roads, no nothing up there at the time . . . when you're a kid you see these things and you remember them.' Bridget and Patrick lived in a small two-up, two-down terraced home at 54 Stannaway Road, off Sundrive Road. Patrick found intermittent employment as a bricklayer in and around Dublin.

On 2 June 1932, Bridget Brown, pregnant with her twelfth child, collapsed in her home and was rushed to hospital. She was in labour for three days. The doctors then decided to use castor oil to induce the birth because the baby boy was positioned in the womb so that his feet would come out first. Family members waited at the hospital in shifts, wondering if Bridget would survive. Doctors told them that it was quite possible that both mother and child might not make it, but Bridget finally gave birth to Christy on 5 June 1932. After the exhausting ordeal, Bridget was sent away to recuperate. Her newborn son remained in the Rotunda, separated from his mother, not because anyone had noticed that anything was wrong with Christy but because it was thought best to reunite mother and child when Bridget was well enough to take him to church to be baptised. Finally, after two weeks, the nuns handed the baby to Bridget. No one knew that Christy had suffocated during the birth and that this would have terrible side effects, with which Christy would have to live for the rest of his life.

At home, as in many large families, the older children were expected to lend a hand in the younger ones' upbringing. In fact, all the Brown children helped to run the home from an early age. As Paddy, the eldest surviving member of the Brown family, explains: 'It doesn't matter if you're a boy or a girl. You look after whoever is coming up behind you, you look out for them, you know. You could be a year older or ten years older, it doesn't matter. One looks after the other.'

Despite the help she got from her children, Bridget had an enormous job in running the household. She had five children and her husband to feed, clothe and take care of on a small income. She sensed something was different about her newborn son but she was not quite sure what the problem was. As the late Mona Byrne, the second daughter of the Brown family (who passed away in 2005), remembered: 'Well, my mother knew all along, she just would not let it be buried . . . you see, when Christy was born, my mother had had an awful lot of babies, she did all the rearing herself, and she knew in her heart and soul that something was wrong with Christy, cause you would put him up in a pram, she would look back maybe after fifteen minutes and he would be slumping down again. He couldn't sit up and she knew it. The more she kept watching, the more she'd see different things.'

Bridget was puzzled. She watched her child carefully and saw that it was as though his body could not support the weight of his head or even its own frame. His muscles continually twisted, except when he was asleep. After a few months, she was distraught and decided to take Christy to be examined by a doctor. Bridget brought Christy to see physicians in various Dublin hospitals for years; but doctors, nurses and specialists had no answers for her. At first, they dismissed her, saying nothing was wrong with her son. Mona Brown remembered Bridget's frustration: 'When she brought him to be checked out, they told her she was a madwoman. They told her she was imagining [that he was disabled]. They just kept telling her he was a slow learner or he was slow at this or slow at that. But she knew. Nobody knew what cerebral palsy was back then.'

In 1930s Ireland, cerebral palsy was difficult for almost any doctor to understand. The name describes a group of chronic conditions affecting body movements, muscle coordination and usually mental function. 'Cerebral' refers to the brain and 'palsy' means a disorder of movement or posture. The cause of cerebral palsy is damage to one or more areas of the brain, usually occurring during foetal development or infancy. Most commonly, this damage is induced either by an injury to the brain (such as may be caused by meningitis), a haemorrhage or lack of oxygen during birth.

Christy's lack of bodily control was more severe than in most cases of cerebral palsy. In some forms of the disease, only the lower limbs are affected; in other forms, only slight contractions and muscle spasms occur (leaving the affected individual with slurred speech and the ability to use their hands or feet to some degree). However, when Christy's condition was finally properly recognised, the clinical diagnosis was double athetosis. About 10 per cent of cerebral-palsy sufferers have athetoid cerebral palsy. In this type of illness, the areas of the brain responsible for processing signals that enable smooth, coordinated movements, as well as maintaining body posture, do not function properly. Damage to these areas may cause a child to develop involuntary, purposeless movements, especially in the face, arms and trunk. These involuntary movements often interfere with speaking, feeding, reaching, grasping and other skills requiring coordinated gestures or actions. Involuntary grimacing or tongue thrusting may lead to swallowing problems, drooling and slurred speech. Often, the movements increase during periods of emotional stress and disappear during sleep. Children with athetoid cerebral palsy often have low muscle tone and difficulty maintaining posture for sitting or walking. Seizures similar to those experienced by epileptics are common.

Christy's partial suffocation at birth had left a lesion on his brain, making 'proper coordinated movement impossible in almost every muscle group in his body', as his doctor and mentor Robert Collis would later write. Unusually, however, the lack of oxygen had affected only that part of the brain which controlled his body, while the area of his brain that controlled his intellect was entirely unharmed. His body was almost useless; his mind was perfect.

As the infant Christy grew and his symptoms became more obvious, doctors admitted that *something* was wrong with him, but they did not know exactly what it was. They told Bridget that he was a 'mental defective'. The only advice they could offer her was to place him into what was then referred to as a 'deaf-and-dumb home'. She refused. As Ann, the youngest daughter of the Brown family, recalls, 'I remember me mammy saying they thought he would be like an imbecile and he wouldn't talk or think or anything. She said, "He was bred in my body and he's not going into a home." There were no social services then but they had this thing, you know, and they were trying to get her, what with so many children in the house, to put him away but she just said no. No, she wouldn't put him away. Sure, what was one more? But she always knew there was something there; she saw that light in his eyes. And she brought out that brightness, that spark. She brought it out.'

In an interview with Brid Mahon, published in the *Sunday Press* in 1962 and entitled 'The Triumph of Mother Courage', Bridget remembered:

> The day that the doctors told me that Christy was mentally defective and should be sent to a home was the darkest day of my life. I pushed the pram, with two babies in it, all the way from the centre of the city to Crumlin, and I was glad it was raining because I cried all the way home. Mind you, I knew Christy was as bright and as intelligent as any of the others . . . I made a vow

that day coming home from the hospital that Christy would lead as normal a life as possible. I promised myself I wouldn't spoil him, but that I would see to it that he was the centre of family life – no pushing him away in the back room. God had given me Christy. Who was I to question his will?

Instead of institutionalising Christy, Bridget tried continually to stimulate him, by playing with him, speaking to him and reading to him as often as she could. She realised she had to engage him both intellectually and physically and she told the older children to do the same. Above all, Bridget wanted Christy's life to be as much like those of other children as possible. His brothers and sisters were expected to speak to him, to play with him and mind him. The presumed 'mental defective' was as much a part of the family as anyone else.

In some respects, Christy was able, even as a child, to take part in the life of the community as well as that of the family. The local children would often take boxes from the local grocer's shop and find some wheels to turn them into carts to race around in. A larger box was sought out for Christy and the best-quality wheels found so that he could be mobile and play with his friends. His brothers took Christy out every day in his 'chariot', as he nicknamed it, to play and wreak general havoc. Bridget also told the *Sunday Press*:

> There's a great comradeship amongst children. His brothers and sisters took him around in the old go-cart. He went on picnics with them to the pine forest. One day they went swimming in the canal, and decided because Christy wanted to, to give him a dip. That nearly killed his father and myself, but Christy enjoyed it.

When Christy's brothers and the rest of the gang in the street stole some fruit or sweets, they used the ultimate hiding place: underneath Christy in his chariot. Paddy Brown remembers: 'You'd be down in the shops in Sundrive Road, you'd be robbing stuff out of the shop and you'd stick it in under your man's arse, under the seats. 'Twas only for the craic. No one would have dreamt of looking. They'd look *into* it, but they'd never take the seat out.'

By listening to his mother reading to him and by spending time with other children, Christy developed his language skills. To onlookers and listeners, what he uttered sounded like gibberish, but his mother always understood her son's grunts and by the time he was seven his siblings began to understand him too. This code, a secret language, became a great bond between him and his family.

Outsiders who met Christy would recount how hard it was to understand him and say that even after his speech therapy (which he did not receive until his teens), it would take several conversations before they began to comprehend his contorted words and uncontrolled voice, the result of muscle spasms from his cerebral palsy. His sister Mona remembered taking Christy out when he was a teenager, perhaps over to the shops or to the local park, and the neighbourhood women would pass by, crossing themselves and saying, 'Ah, sure, bless the poor lad,' or they would speak to Mona and then look down at Christy, raising their voices and speaking very slowly, saying, 'Hi, Christy, nice day, love, eh?'

'Fucking auld ones. Fuck off!' he would mutter at them. Mona always tried not to laugh and hoped the neighbours had not understood what Christy had called them.

Many years later, when Christy was famous, he was asked to meet with Peter Sellers and Britt Ekland. He went to see them and after having spent only fifteen minutes in their company, he turned to his sister Ann and said, 'These people are awful wankers.' Sellers (who had ignored Christy after their initial introduction) leant over to Christy's 'interpreter' and asked, somewhat pedantically, 'What's that he's saying?' Ann did not know what to say, so she thought quickly. 'Ah, sure, I don't know,' she said. 'He's speaking Irish.'

By the time Christy was five, Bridget was convinced that despite her son's very serious problems, he was not a 'simple boy'. Doctors had offered little hope, telling her that he would probably never walk or talk, let alone lead an independent life, but Bridget refused to give up on her son and the bond between them grew as they faced more and more obstacles. She and Christy were becoming almost telepathically linked, as the rest of the family noticed. Mona remembered how Bridget 'was the only one who could control him, and that was without violence or anything'. Patrick Brown was working six or seven days a week as a bricklayer to support his family and he made sure he found a job in Kimmage so that he could help take care of Christy. Every morning, he took him to the toilet, washed him and fed him his breakfast. Christy was unable to hold a fork or spoon; sometimes his jaw would lock for several minutes at a time and his food had to be cut into tiny pieces to prevent him from choking if he had a convulsion while eating. Patrick was resigned to his son's disability, seeing him simply as someone who required care but believing that Christy would always be unable to look after himself, always be dependent on them. Bridget, however, thought differently. She continued to take Christy to clinics and hospitals to be poked and prodded and no doubt gaped at – both she and he humiliated – but she always returned without any solutions.

A young doctor, Patricia Epstein, was working in the outpatients department at Harcourt Street Children's Hospital in Dublin in 1937, when Christy was brought before her and several other doctors to be assessed. In an article written for the *Irish Times* in 1970, Epstein remembered the dignity with which Bridget Brown carried herself and the tenderness with which she treated her child. According to her, Bridget walked into the hospital with a proud carriage and her head held high. She was wrapped from head to toe in a long black shawl and waited patiently to be seen. When called to come into the examination room, she sat down in front of the waiting doctors, took off her shawl and revealed Christy, to audible intakes of breath and murmurs of astonishment. Dr Epstein wondered if any of them had seen a child come into the hospital who was 'so grossly deformed'. Christy appeared crumpled, like a collapsed old doll whose stuffing was falling out. His tiny arms and emaciated legs were flexed against his body so that his knees touched his chin. All his arms and legs were distorted, shaped into something irregular and unnatural; they were as rigid as if he had rigor mortis. Atop his broken and fragile frame sat his head, which, because of his fractured body, appeared enormous.

Bridget ignored the doctors' obvious shock. She undressed Christy slowly and with enormous patience, because his muscle spasms and flailing limbs made moving and clothing him very difficult. She kissed him sweetly and gently, reassuring him as she removed each garment. Their eye contact was unwavering.

The day Dr Epstein met Bridget, she felt something positive had to be said to her and they discussed the fact that the big toe on Christy's left foot was mobile. Bridget left the hospital not having heard the term 'cerebral palsy' but still determined not to give up hope for her child. Not only did they read together every day but she would sing Irish songs to him in front of the fire for hours when most of the others were out. Finally, when Christy was only five, he rewarded his mother's faith one December night in 1937. The Brown family were gathered round the kitchen fire in their small front room. Mona and Paddy were doing homework on an old chipped slate, writing with a piece of yellow chalk. Christy sat propped up on a stack of pillows watching them.

At first, he was interested in their work and conversation. Then he noticed the chalk they were using. He wrote later: 'I was fascinated by it as much as if it had been a stick of gold.' Without understanding what he was doing, he reached out and took the stick of chalk with his left foot, between his first and second toe, and drew a small line. He watched as his foot seemed to move as if of its own volition. He recalled later that having made just that small scribble with the chalk, he felt dazed and unsure of what to do next. He looked up and saw his father watching intently from beside the fire.

Just then, Bridget walked in from the kitchen and saw the children's stares. Then she noticed the chalk held in Christy's left foot. She put down the pot she was carrying, crossed the floor and knelt down beside her son.

'I'll show you what to do,' she told him, and she wrote the capital letter 'A' on the slate. 'Copy that,' she told him.

He could not. His muscles would not work for him; he grasped at the chalk with his toes but could not move it.

'Try again,' Bridget urged.

He managed a small line.

She whispered to him, 'Again.'

He wrote another line and the chalk broke. He sank his teeth into his lips, pressed his fingernails into his palms and connected the lines. The lines formed the letter 'A'.

Thirty years later, Christy wrote a poem for his mother, to be read at her funeral. He wrote to one of his closest friends, just after finishing it:

> Thank you for today . . . I need such days so much . . . when one stands constantly too close to a bright light one is more apt to get blinded; likewise when darkness – of any kind – is one's constant companion the danger of blindness is equally apparent. In my time I have suffered from both kinds of blindness, and cannot say one is preferable to the other . . . here at last is the requiem for my mother I promised you. A poor effort, God knows. Yet, in her rare indefinable way she might have said 'not bad'.

This is part of the poem he composed for her:

For My Mother
With gay uplifted finger you beckoned
        and faltering I followed you down paths
I would not otherwise have known or dared
        limping after you up that secret mountain
where you sang without need of voice or words.
        I touched briefly the torch you held out
And bled pricked by a thorn from the black deep rose of
                your courage.
        From the gutter of my defeated dreams
you pulled me to heights almost your own.

    Only in your dying, Lady, could I offer you a poem.

I do not grieve for you
        in your little pot of indiscriminate clay
for now you shall truly dance

O great heart
  O best of all my songs
    the dust be merciful upon your holy bones.

When asked to choose their favourite piece of Christy's work, this is the poem his brothers and sisters most often name.

What Bridget Brown did not know on that day when her son wrote the letter 'A' in front of his family was that Christy would go on to become a bestselling writer, a celebrity, and that her work and her faith in him would be rewarded tenfold.

Chapter Three

~~~~~~

A LETTER

It sounds wildly contradictory, I know, but my life is still essentially quite lonely and isolated, even with such a large family about me, and this kind of loneliness (mental and in a non-religious way, spiritual, rather than physical) can be very awful and dangerous, if one has any receptivity and sensitivity whatsoever, and God only knows I have more than my fair share of both. It is a barrier, however impalpable, that was there from the start, and it has grown bigger in time, and this inevitable loneliness, living in a vacuum, in the very midst of activity and restless life, has me driven to mad acts in my longing to approach them and absorb myself in their lives . . .

Have you any old – but good – books you can give to Ann for me? I remember you said you had lots of books that you never got round to reading, and I could do with some fresh reading material – the sort of stuff it's not easy to come by in this holy and green land of ours. In particular if you've any Scott Fitzgerald or Graham Greene they'd be very welcome, but I'd be thankful for anything you think I'd enjoy on those sleepless nights that come all too often now. Hope life is reasonably endurable for you. That's all any of us can hope for.

Chris

Christy Brown, writing to his brother Seán,
3 September 1973

Christy's disability meant he spent countless days sitting in the family home listening to and watching the people of Kimmage from the front window. Images of birds (particularly hawks) are constantly used throughout his work, because they symbolise his position as the outsider quietly observing from afar. Although his mother and siblings had done everything they could to help him integrate into the world, it was inevitable that as he grew into early adolescence he would feel isolated and left alone. In his life, Christy Brown would write over a thousand letters, a memoir (a bestseller in three countries), four novels (one of which was a bestseller in fifteen countries) and four collections of poetry; he would also produce hundreds of paintings; all would reflect how his isolation would create a great observer of the human spirit.

On a normal day in 1937, in the small Brown family home in Kimmage at 54 Stannaway Road, Christy's intelligence had been demonstrated in only the most simple way – by his writing the letter 'A'. As he wrote in *My Left Foot*, he had found the chalk and its colour utterly compelling. The bright-yellow stick had seemed to draw him to it as opposed to the other way round. It had taken superhuman strength for Christy just to hold between his toes the small stub of chalk he had taken from his sister Mona and grasp it long enough to scrawl two simple angled lines with a squiggle in between. Bridget had wondered in quiet moments of despair if her faith would ever be rewarded and she had asked God for help: 'inwardly, she prayed God would give some proof of her faith. She knew it was one thing to believe, but quite another thing to prove,' Christy recalled in his memoir.

Once, when he was five years old, Bridget had sat reading with Christy for hours before putting him to sleep. She read aloud to him from a baby's book, telling him about the elephants, chickens and pigs. Afterwards, she put the book down, stroked his head and asked him, 'Did you enjoy that, Christy? Wasn't that nice reading about the animals?' She smiled at him. 'Will you nod your head "yes"? Nod your head "yes" like a good boy for me.' She was desperate for him to show a sign that he might one day be able to communicate with the outside world. His face grimaced and twisted; then his hands reached out and grasped the curls sitting about her neck, locking themselves on her hair – this often happened during his convulsions. She delicately diffused his tight muscles, spoke softly to him and cajoled him into bed. She then walked away into the small, dimly gas-lit hallway and cried.

For more than five years, others had believed that both she and Christy were fools and Bridget had worried that her son would be trapped in silence forever. She was a staunchly religious woman; now her vigil had been rewarded. Her main concern had been what would happen to Christy after she and Patrick were dead and the rest of the children had families of their own. Now that she knew for certain Christy heard her and understood her, she yearned for him to be literate. She knew that if he could write and express himself, there was less danger in his being left alone and unprotected; without being able to write and tell people what he needed, he was completely vulnerable. So she began to devote her time to helping him learn to read and write. Together they began to tackle the alphabet, letter by letter. Christy was not a slow learner, as the doctors had told her. His appetite for knowledge was voracious.

By now Bridget had seven children to care for. Lizzie, the eldest, was nicknamed 'Titch'. Both she and Mona (the second daughter) helped Bridget with the upkeep of their home and with caring for Christy. The eldest boy, Tony, was beginning to look for work, while Jim and Paddy were in school and the newest addition to the family, Peter, was only a baby. Christy and Bridget would spend hours working together; whenever she had free time, she devoted it to helping him. At first, she would write single letters on the stone floor of the house, which had been worn down with so many people walking on it. She would show Christy how to make the shapes and help him to begin memorising them. She would then wipe the letter away with an old duster and wait for him to write it. In time, he learned to hold the chalk quite steadily between his big toe and his second toe. His mother would get on with the housework and once he had completed a task, he would howl for her to come and see if he had done it correctly. 'If I was wrong,' he wrote in *My Left Foot*, 'I'd make her kneel down, her hands covered with flour, and show me the right way to do it.'

This informal method of learning was the only real instruction Christy Brown received. There was nowhere in Dublin or even in Ireland where someone with Christy's illness could be taught. Many years later, he would be criticised for his verbosity and for the lack of structure and awareness of grammar in his writing. He was indeed unaware of these things. Never in his life did he have an English teacher, nor did he ever attend a proper course in literature or language. In fact, in his late twenties, Christy tried to earn a degree through the British Open University but he did not complete it. This was not because he lacked the intellect but rather because his means of learning was erratic and unstructured. For him, it was a case of learning by ear – it was a necessity for his survival. Throughout his life, his appetite for books was insatiable but he was never compelled to study literature in a formal way. His first five years were spent in almost total silence and he was never able to read his own work aloud, which meant that his understanding of language was fractured on the simplest level.

However, Christy understood sound and language in an uncanny way. His form of communication existed in a world of rearranged boundaries: uttered speech was irrelevant, writing was quintessential to being understood and, above all, listening was paramount. This unique circumstance would create a style that focused on the individual's voice so that vivid characters and their stories came to the fore of each narrative Christy wrote. For those who read his stories and poems, the experience is akin to listening to the inner dialogue of someone's mind, rather than reading words spoken to them as is the experience with most novels. Christy Brown's voice as a writer was a torrent of inner thinking and feeling which piled word on word; paragraphs were pages in his work. Yet, for all his writings and the success and recognition he received, he never felt as though he was really heard, or perhaps listened to. From this well of frustration, another torrent came forth: a stream of anger which underpinned his work and personal life and from which no one was safe, including Christy himself.

After working with his mother for many hours, which turned into weeks and months, Christy finally conquered the alphabet and embarked upon the colossal task of learning how to put the letters together. He had become bored of drawing individual letters and wanted to use the characters to form words, and not just basic words. His first achievement was writing his initials. Often he would place them in the wrong order (B.C.) and become infuriated. A strong temper reared its head whenever he failed at these small attempts at writing. He would throw the chalk across the room or onto the floor in disgust. His mother would simply pick it up and give it back to him quietly, shaming him into trying again. This was a technique Bridget often used to cope with Christy's frustration. She was always patient and would use her soft voice and calm demeanour to tame his tantrums. He persevered and became enormously proud of his accomplishments.

For weeks after he had written and practised his initials, he would look at his immediate surroundings, see a chair, for example, and attempt to write the word. If he wrote it incorrectly, he would spit on the floor, rub the word away with his heel and begin again. His first pieces of written vocabulary came from the front room of the house in Kimmage. He could write 'chair', 'fire', 'door' and so on. These challenges soon became too simple. Yet he realised that this ability not only pleased his mother but gave her enormous pride.

Previously, only his mother could fully understand his

strange grunts. Now, he finally had the power to tell his family what he wanted to say. He would write on the worn slate whatever he was trying to express. His ability to write seemed to change his character: he had sat and passively observed for a long, long time and now, as he learned to speak, he had a very strong voice and many words he wanted to enunciate.

His left foot was also becoming more than something to write with; he was using it to do almost everything. Bridget abhorred the fact that he never wore shoes or slippers; she felt it made him look 'very much neglected', as his brother Paddy recalls. But whenever she put shoes or socks on his feet, he quickly kicked them off. He would write that with his feet covered he 'felt as any normal person might feel if his hands were tied behind his back'. His left foot was gradually becoming indispensable to him. It was developing into the equivalent of most people's right hand. He would eventually achieve such dexterity with his left foot that he could play the piano for his family, having learned the songs by ear. Christy's brother Paddy remembers: 'He'd be learning off you all the time . . . with the chalk between his toes, and he'd be writing. 'Twas like a miracle to see him. I still don't know how he done it. Eating a cut of bread, and that food was able to come up to here [pointing to his mouth]. Do you know what I mean? And further up! He was like a contortionist.'

One day, a doctor came to see one of Christy's brothers, who had sprained his wrist. The doctor said goodbye to Bridget and then noticed Christy sitting on the floor by the table writing with his left foot, as he often did, positioned so that he was out of everyone's way, with his back against the wall so he could put his weight onto the lower part of his body and focus on carefully balancing a pencil in his left foot. The doctor, as Christy wrote:

> was very incredulous. He began to ask mother questions about me and, being anxious to show him that I understood all that was being said . . . she . . . invited

him to ask me to write something for him. He thought for a moment, then he took out his big report ledger from his bag, offered me a big red pencil and asked me to write my name in the book.

I took the pencil between my toes, pulled the book toward me, steadied myself, and slowly wrote my name on the fly-leaf in big block-letter capitals.

'Amazing! I'm astonished, Mrs Brown.'

The neighbours in Kimmage were also astonished and often came to the Brown family home to watch Christy write. However, he had privately decided on another display of his talents. He sat alone for weeks secretly working on a new word he had found in Paddy's schoolbook. It was now April 1939 and he had been learning to write for almost a year and a half. In the early twilight, Bridget sat by the fire, nursing her baby, Eamonn. The rest of the children were upstairs playing school. Christy sat with a pencil between his toes, slumped into the couch, his back supported by a huge stack of pillows. He kept on trying to write a particular word but could not get it right. He wanted to cry out for his mother as he always did but as he watched her nursing her child, he concentrated harder and did not tell anyone that he needed help. Eventually, he called out for her. Bridget chastised him, telling him he would wake the baby. He grunted more loudly and she knew she had to go over to him. 'New word, is it?' she asked. He smiled, picked up the pencil and methodically wrote in the margin of a book the word which had been plaguing him for weeks. He looked up at Bridget. She was staring at the word 'mother'. She looked at the word silently, not moving or saying anything for several minutes. She then turned and looked at him, placed her hand on his shoulder and smiled. Christy was six years old.

For several years, Christy joined in with his brothers' and sisters' boisterous games while he also worked on his reading and on writing small words and phrases. Then, one day, when he was ten years old, his chariot broke. The axle snapped and the seat had worn out. 'Henry', as Christy had called it, was put in the coal shed to rust. His brothers and sisters were getting older and developing an interest in the opposite sex, going out and becoming more independent. Christy felt left behind and a dark cloud that had been hanging in his subconscious was spreading; it would eventually emerge as a thunderous storm.

Even when he was very young, he had had a 'queer idea that there was something wrong'. Now, something was starting to dawn on him and it 'loomed larger' in his mind the more he wrote. His new capacity to write was linked to his beginning to understand his otherness. As he learned to express himself, communicating meant processing the world around him and all the differences in that world. Now he knew that he was not the same as other people and he started to imagine the impact this difference would have on his life. After this realisation, Christy did not go outside and would not play with his brothers and sisters and the gang from the Sundrive Road area. For the next two years, he would stay indoors, write and think, trying to hide from the world. Like Hamlet, he knew that inadequacy would stem from his paralysis. Ironically, it was not the physical inertia that upset him but the mental paralysis that came from his now knowing how disabled he was. His mother had succeeded so adeptly in immersing him in family life and treating him as normal that Christy had not known just how serious his condition was until he began to write.

Initially, he could not fathom the difference between himself and others. He could only grasp that it was there and that it was important. One day, he began to stare at the hands of his brother Peter; they were brown and muscular. He compared them with his own hands, which he thought were more like 'claws' – bound like twine in tight bunches. In *My Left Foot*, he remembered:

> Now I was seldom happy. I'd sit at the window in the kitchen and gaze out at my brothers and their pals as

they played a football match on the road outside the house . . . Sometimes some of them would smile and wave in at me. I'd try to wave back, but when I lifted my arm it would shoot out sideways and bang against the window-frame. Then I'd throw myself on to the sofa behind me and bury my face in the corner of it.

What Christy did not know was that he had been given a gift: he would from that time on understand the dire human condition of loneliness. He would create characters who, although they were not disabled, were profoundly alone in some way; he would see desperation in everyone he met and convey to his readers how the simple act of living was a challenge for everyone. Another gift took seed here as well: he was learning how to become a fighter – and not to care what other people thought of him.

By 1942, at the age of ten, Christy had begun to hate mirrors. He had never before been aware of the differences between other people and himself. Now, when he looked in the mirror, he saw grotesqueness. His twisted face, with its drooling mouth, and his broken hands were repugnant to him; he was disgusted by his reflection. Christy wrote that this was when he realised that he was only a 'spectator' living outside the realms of normal life. One night, Bridget heard an enormous clatter coming from the upstairs bedroom where Christy had been working. When she went up to the room and opened the door, she found him lying amongst pieces of shattered glass. He had struck out at the mirror with his left foot. 'That's seven years' bad luck,' she told him, and she threw away the broken mirror.

Bridget was watching her son carefully and constantly. While he had been growing slowly more depressed, she had been saving every penny she could from her housekeeping to buy him a wheelchair. The day after he got the new chair, he was taken outside to play with the boys, who became very excited and started suggesting names for the new chariot. Christy could not look at the people around him. He hated every stare. When he passed strangers, he tried to hide his hands as best he could and push his face towards his shoulder, slumping down and avoiding all eye contact. He wrote, 'After that day I went out no more, except, perhaps, once or twice a year, and even then I'd only let them take me out to quiet lonely places where there were no houses or people.'

The only thing from which he derived any pleasure was copying from newspapers with a lead pencil held between his toes. However, while copying was fine, Christy still had no real means of self-expression and the pressure of living day to day in a type of prison was building inside him. He found himself in another cage – not just a cage of silence but a new and more sinister one created by his otherness. He would later write to his brother Seán in London, in the letter which opens this chapter:

> I know all too well how easy it is to get depressed . . . it is a very frightening and terrifying experience, courting passionately with the idea of death, it is also the essence of both cowardice and selfishness. I am speaking now out of personal experience over the years when I felt absolutely alone, useless, a failed and flawed thing, when the nothingness of myself was a daily spectre I had to face and live with in bleak coexistence, when it was a daily miracle to survive, let alone live.

Chapter Four

A FRIENDSHIP

I want to emphasise how deeply thankful I am for you being so good to me. You are so angelic that I feel like a heel. It is more than ever important to me that I should have you near, for I am having one of those difficult emotional periods which we like to imagine we left behind in our adolescence. Those which remain with us on and off throughout life, and the more sensitive and imaginative we are the more often we suffer like this. You understand so much in such a quiet and deep felt way, there is no need for me to explain or indulge in histrionics with you. You are very very good for me. God knows I don't deserve you.

There is so little I can do to show my affection, my thanks or my love. It is one of the grandest things in life to have someone to turn to when one tethers on the brink of a great pain. It is so important to have this deep cool reservoir of understanding and faith with this one person. You fulfil that function in my life and always have. I know such a sense of peace with you, there is seldom need for words. They are almost superfluous. The thought of not having you there is unthinkable. It just never occurs to me. I will always need you in my life and it seems only natural that you should always be there. It is not arrogance or conceit or taking anything for granted; if it is anything at all I would call it faith.

Christy Brown, writing to Katriona Maguire,
April 1965

Christy Brown met Katriona Delahunt (later Maguire) in 1943, when his mother had just given birth to her last child, Danny. Bridget was very ill after the birth and was told she must stay in the Rotunda Hospital for several weeks to recover. Katriona was working as a Lady Almoner at the hospital. Essentially, the Almoners were the first social workers in Ireland. Katriona became involved in medical social work as one of the first students at the newly founded University College Dublin, taking a diploma in social science (two years after she began her studies, the diploma became an official degree course). When she finished her course, she became involved in a project that was run by Dr Robert Collis.

Collis was a paediatrician from a wealthy Anglo-Irish family. His interests lay not only in medicine but also in improving the social conditions of Dublin. He and the Quaker businessman Victor Bewley founded an organisation which they named the Marrowbone Lane Fund, after a street in Dublin. Its purpose was to help provide the poor working-class children of the city's tenements with food and medicine. Conditions in the first decades of the twentieth century in Dublin were deplorable. Many children suffered from rickets, because they could not get enough nutritious food and therefore proper nourishment. As Kevin C. Kearns points out in his book, *Dublin Tenement Life: An Oral History*:

> In the 1930s the poor of inner-city Dublin lived in appalling conditions. In 1934, eleven families with fifty-three members were found to be living in one tenement . . . Two years later a report spoke of five families with twenty-five members living in six rooms in a tenement in Marrowbone Lane and another thirty-three people living in the same number of rooms.

Katriona did not spend time only with the Browns (by whom she eventually became adopted as an honorary family member) but also with other families living on the outskirts of the city and in the inner city. As he watched her work, Collis recognised in Katriona a great character; he saw her as an intelligent, sensitive and diplomatic woman who could help his foundation enormously. Thus he asked her to be the official social worker for the Marrowbone Lane Fund.

The publication of Collis's first autobiography, *The Silver Fleece*, in 1936 had led him to meet the leaders of Irish literary thought. He was a friend of the writer Frank O'Connor, who once told Collis that when he was writing he was 'ever trying to reach the last output of himself' and that it was only when he was 'walking up and down crying out and even weeping to himself' that he was sure he had reached his goal. In 1939, Collis complained to O'Connor that no one in the upper echelons of Dublin society was paying attention to the terrible conditions in the tenements. O'Connor, who was on the board of directors of the Abbey Theatre, turned to Collis and said, 'If you feel so strongly about the Dublin slums, why don't you write us a play about it, then?' A few days later, Collis sat down to write the play at ten o'clock at night; he was finished by morning. *Marrowbone Lane* (produced by Hilton Edwards and Micheál Mac Liammóir at the Gate Theatre) would have a profound effect on the visions people had about the social conditions of the inner city at the time. It was reviewed positively and was a popular play with Irish audiences. So Collis achieved what he wanted: Dublin tenement life and its horrors became a topic of debate in the media and in politics. In the first edition of the printed version of the play, Collis wrote in his Introduction:

> In 1925, the world was very sick. In the 'have' states a very middle class was living in freedom, the meaning of which they understood as freedom to exploit. They felt little, if any, responsibility to society . . . So in America Steinbeck, seeing the big monopolists driving the small man to the wall and destroying the family, started to write 'The Grapes of Wrath'. In England [Walter] Greenwood,

seeing uncontrolled individual enterprise degrading and dehumanising England's splendid stock, commenced to work on his moving indictment of unemployment 'Love on the Dole'.

Here in Ireland, the present author, moved by the same impulse, sat down one night and began the dialogue of 'Marrowbone Lane'. The idea was simple enough. Here in Dublin lived two societies, one of which did not know how the other lived – did not know that 90,000 people lived in one-roomed tenements and 10,000 dwellings condemned as medically unfit for human habitation. Still less did they realise what this meant in pain, disease, cold and hunger. They did not know that children were daily turned away from the hospitals to die in their mothers' arms or in cold cots in damp, dirty, smelly slums. Most did not know, and those who did either didn't care or felt it was no business of theirs anyway . . . the story of Marrowbone Lane is being re-enacted again and again in the dirty slums of the city, but all the same, there is a new feeling in men's hearts which I believe will find expression in years to come. Reforms may arrive slowly, but they are coming, and if we can bring them about in such a way as to raise the material standard of life without forgetting the needs of the soul, we can build a society in this our beloved Island which may yet be the envy of the world.

Katriona Delahunt had similar altruistic ideals and wanted to make a difference in her community. When Bridget Brown first met her in 1943, she liked the young social worker instantly. Katriona asked Bridget if there was anything she could do to help her, because she seemed so exhausted and was required to stay in the hospital for several weeks to recover after the birth. Bridget asked her if she would please go and check on the twelve children she had at home in Kimmage. She said she would, of course, and so the next day she cycled to 54 Stannaway Road.

The first time Katriona saw Christy Brown, he was sitting under the bay window in the front room of the Brown family home, propped up by pillows and working at his writing, as Katriona would often find him in the years to come. When she said hello, the reply she heard from him was incomprehensible. She introduced herself to the whole family and gave sweets to the children, as would become her habit. She then sat and spoke with Christy's father, Patrick, telling him about Bridget's condition and when she was expected to come home from the hospital. She decided she would like to come back to the house and visit again, and so she asked Mr Brown if he would let her do so. All the Brown family, father and children alike, were thrilled – after meeting Katriona only once they adored her. To this day, the surviving members of the Brown family still call Katriona 'Ms Maguire'.

As Katriona remembers: 'Christy's mother had brought him to various doctors but nobody, no one, had any solutions. They just said, "Put him in a nursing home." I just happened to be working for Dr Collis as a social worker. I was looking after children in the charity [the Marrowbone Lane Fund] I worked for. Dr Collis set up a smallish committee and he had a couple of businessmen get involved. One of them was Victor Bewley, the owner of Bewley's Café. He was an extraordinary man. He gave us the use of his restaurant every night when it closed, every evening at half past five. I was responsible for picking up the children, his staff stayed on and they served the children a very good, well-balanced meal. These were all children from the children's hospital . . . I remember at the Savoy Cinema at Christmas there used to be tea and a film for the children. Dr Collis came out there and he saw Christy and took a great interest in him. At that stage, he would have been about fifteen or sixteen. Afterwards, Christy was taken to Dr Collis's clinic down in Harcourt Street. When I first met Christy, though, he was only able to kind of grunt. He was a very frail boy and, naturally, he couldn't walk.'

After Bridget came back from the hospital, Katriona continued to call over to the Browns, always bringing gifts for the children. She was very interested in Christy and asked Bridget many questions about his condition and the assistance they had received from doctors and the social system. Bridget told her that she had really not had help from anyone, that she had been told that Christy should be put into a home. Christy was not in a good emotional state when Katriona began visiting the Browns. He was often withdrawn and quiet. Bridget recounted the story of the day when he had picked up a piece of chalk and written the letter 'A' and Katriona began to spend time with Christy working on his reading and writing. She found his personality and tenacity admirable and wanted to spend as much time with him as she could. The other children had school to educate them; Christy had his mother and Katriona.

Communicating with him was the problem. Katriona had to learn to understand what he was saying: 'In the beginning it was extremely difficult but I got used to it. His mother was often there with me, you know; she was in the kitchen and there was a round table in the room and Christy would sit on the table and do his reading and writing and painting. And she'd know I was stuck, she'd know I didn't understand a word, and she'd gently fill it in without making any fuss over it. Later, I'd ask Christy to keep on saying it and if I still couldn't make him out then I'd just say, "I can't understand you."'

Slowly, Katriona grew to understand Christy's speech and an intimate bond was formed between the two, a friendship which would last for forty-one years. Katriona watched, astonished, as Christy painted and wrote: 'He learned to read because his mother had done the alphabet on the floor. I used to bring him basic children's books and sometimes we used to read the headlines of the *Evening Herald*. He just soaked it up and in no time at all he was reading everything and anything. It was a wonderful thing when he started to write. In the beginning, he wrote with his big toe and the toe next to it, with a pen, for hours. I remember seeing him paint a New York scene and he couldn't reach up to the top skyscraper in the painting so he just flipped it upside down with his left foot and finished it just like that. It was perfect.'

On Christmas Day 1942, Christy's elder brother Paddy had been given a box of paints. Christy was desperate for them. He offered Paddy a swap for the lead soldiers he had got for Christmas. Christy's brother was more than happy to oblige. After that, Paddy remembers, it was 'an awful lot of painting – paints, paints . . . It wasn't so much writing at the time, it was painting.'

This avid painting continued and Christy's father made him a special box in which to store his paints, which he named his 'toolbox'. Painting day after day was the perfect way for Christy to release his pent-up emotions. Writing took a great deal of time and effort; it required books, asking questions of his family and Katriona, and for his mother or his siblings to check his spelling. Painting allowed him a private space where no one could tell him that he was right or wrong and he was left in his own creative world to express himself. Katriona Delahunt served as his only real critic and all she did was tell him how amazing his work was. This encouraged him but her sentiment was genuine: she was always impressed by his work.

One afternoon in 1944, he noticed an advert in an issue of a national newspaper. The *Sunday Independent* was running a painting competition for children aged twelve to sixteen in Dublin. Christy was excited and worked hard on one particular canvas. His mother suggested that he enter, telling him he didn't have to be the best but why not try? After finishing the painting, he didn't want to enter because he thought he had no chance of winning. His mother tried to persuade him to submit the painting, but he refused. Yet when Katriona told him he should send it in, as he wrote later, 'I couldn't refuse to do whatever my "dream-girl" asked me.' Christy won and the newspaper sent photographers to take pictures of him; when they found out that he had painted the picture with his left foot, it became a great story to run – for the first but not the last time in his life. The journalist could not believe that he had painted the work with his foot and he stared as Bridget helped her son to get set up and he watched Christy paint.

Later, in 1950, Christy wrote to Katriona:

> . . . it would be so easy for me to be merely grateful to you, but my nature is not placid enough for that; my convictions about life go too deeply for me to experience such a facile emotion as gratitude about something which is so deeply embedded in my life. I was so afraid that you would stop coming to see me, that it was really most heroic of me to even try and describe my feelings to you; and indeed the word 'emotions' is quite wrong, for it has a certain air of inconstancy and brevity about it which is absolutely out of keeping with what is in my mind and heart about you.
>
> One can feel emotion about a beautiful sunset or a piece of music, and yet forget them entirely as they die away. One can feel like that with people too and forget them with equal ease. There are so many shades and grades of certainty and certitude about human feeling, so many sublimations and idealisations of human love, that you are terribly open to doubt and suspicion if you should speak too prodigally of 'Love' . . . there is so much to love in life . . . do you think I will ever be a poet? That is what I want to be more than anything else, for to me life is extraordinarily beautiful, and I want to sing about it, but at times I feel like a bird trapped in a cage without wings or voice.

Their friendship endured because, as Christy said himself, after his mother, she was his 'greatest inspiration in the years and struggles' he had to face. Katriona always treated Christy as a person with a disability rather than as a disabled person. Throughout his life, he always confided in her, telling her about his love affairs, hopes and dreams. As she read to Christy, listened to his thoughts about the world and gave books and paints to him, he came out of his shell. Whenever Christy entered into a severe depression, in which he felt alone and muted (he would later write a poem with the title 'Muted'), he turned to Katriona for solace. After Christy had known her for only a short while, he fell in love with her and throughout the early years of his life, and indeed for the rest of it, part of his heart belonged to Katriona Delahunt. They had, he wrote in *My Left Foot*, 'a strange unconscious language of our own, a peculiar way of understanding each other without consciously expressing ourselves'.

At the age of twelve, Christy was not only beginning to express himself in his paintings but also to express himself sexually. A young girl in Kimmage called Jenny took an interest in him. Unlike the other girls in the neighbourhood, Jenny was not scared of Christy. He thought she was wild and beautiful and bold, and she was also fascinated by him. In *My Left Foot*, Jenny is portrayed as a young love, a crush that would be a natural part of growing up. They exchange short love letters, and a stolen kiss. In Christy's first novel, *Down All the Days* (his second book, not published until 1970), however, the description of the 'love' between a bold young girl, Maureen, and the Christy character is quite different. In the latter work, he writes that one day Maureen approached the boy as he sat in his go-cart, eyed him carefully and then crawled into the box-car and stared him straight in the eyes. He stared back at her, terrified, as he felt her hand crawl slowly up his thigh. She spoke aloud to herself, saying, 'I often thought . . . don't be afraid now . . . are you like the rest?' Then she laughed as she felt his erection and, still looking him in the eye, defiantly declared, 'Just like all the fucking rest!'

By the age of thirteen, he was aware of his sexuality and of his difference to others. By eighteen, this had not changed. And so Christy Brown's aesthetic was always linked to a rebellious attitude – a compulsion to challenge the norm and ignore rules of censorship and what should be written or painted. His favourite artists included Egon Schiele and Tennessee Williams, both of whom he copied and neither of whom would tolerate self-censorship in their art.

Adrian Dunbar, the BAFTA-nominated screenwriter and actor, whose film work includes parts in *The Crying Game* and *The General* and in *My Left Foot* as Katriona Maguire's husband, remarks that Christy's work reminds him of 'a really precocious adolescent . . . my feeling about him is that, no matter who you are or what you are, you have to go through your adolescence, and everything that is difficult in your life comes up in your adolescence, so when he first found his capacity to communicate, I believe those were the things he was interested in, things that young people, people under the age of twenty, are really interested in . . . He absolutely gets that "You-don't-know-what-I'm-thinking!" thing and that is an adolescent thing. Every teenager gets to that point where he talks to the adults around him, saying, you know, "You don't understand what you're talking about. You don't know what I'm thinking. You saying you can read my mind now?" And he has that quality in his work. All the time, he is coming from that place where one person is saying to the other person, "You don't really know what's going on in my head."'

Having read one of Christy's plays (unpublished and never performed), Dunbar believes it would still strike a chord with 'every teenager in Ireland'. To be disenfranchised, to feel isolated and unheard, was what Christy understood. In the play, a young man (aged roughly seventeen) passes by a woman at a first-floor window and starts a conversation with her. She invites him up and they sit and talk, and he is enthralled and yet somehow appalled by this older woman. As they drink, the young man throws existential musings her way, quoting philosophers and poets in an attempt to spar intellectually with the woman and impress her.

Dunbar says, 'I really liked the play . . . because of its adolescent shifts. He is dirty, he's angry, he's obsessed with sexuality, he's . . . bitter about things. His young protagonist is like a *clochard*, you know, he's scruffy, he's dirty, he's bare. I think as a cipher for understanding the pain of teenage years, this is some of the best stuff I have ever seen. This kid who he writes about in this play who comes and sees this woman who is a few years older – not much but a few, you know, you imagine he might be seventeen and she twenty-four or something like this, which in those years, to him, would have been absolutely huge – the terrible thing about it is that the girl is trapped in stasis and he is a young man disaffected on the fringes . . . she is trying to create a space where affection might rear its ugly head and he keeps pushing it away but in the end he feels redeemed and walks out almost with a kind of spring in his step, whereas she is the one who hasn't been so secure in who she is, in handling him, so she ends up thinking maybe I should take a dose of sleeping tablets and end the whole bloody thing. So it's extremely dark and real and very modern, and it is just a little bit overwritten here and there . . . His play, I thought, with a few trims and a few things taken out that are a bit cocky, should be performed in every school in the country, it's so good. If somehow you've been stopped from being able to communicate or you can't communicate how you feel, when it does come out, it *all* comes out . . . For me, all I know, when I read this stuff now, is if I had read this when I was seventeen or eighteen, it would have made a huge impression on me.'

Dunbar's observation is astute in that, without knowing any real detail about Christy's life, he instantly understood from reading the play that the adult Christy, the mature artist, was always affected by his adolescence – or his lack of it. In a letter to Katriona, dated 9 March 1966, Christy wrote:

It is basically a question of being humble, I suppose, and 'putting up' and 'making do' with what one has. And I have never been a very 'humble' person. In a way I suppose I have never really reached adulthood or matured very much since my early years, there is the same fervent searching after love, the same impossible hopes and delusions, the same illogical but unquenchable belief that someday, somewhere, somehow, I will meet the woman who will love me and be everything to me . . . not so much the end of the search as the beginning of a greater adventure. Having the same human needs, desires and longings as other men, but being born with so many physical barriers to thwart and frustrate those drives, would appear the cruellest fate. I sometimes ask myself if it would not have been kinder had God not given me this super-sensitive heart, this intense capacity to imagine happiness and fulfilment. Surely downright imbecility and retardation would have been preferable to this ceaseless agony of heart, mind and body? But inwardly, I know the answer already, and it is a very loud NO! I cannot help being what I am, and I don't think I would anyhow. Being so vulnerable both to joy and sadness has made me what I am . . .

Chapter Five

A DIAGNOSIS

You know, I would very much like to speak, to live an ordinary life, to work, go away, to Texas, see the Amazon, see Broadway, go to Rome, see the Vatican, the Pope! Hey! Did I say an ordinary life? Who do I think I am anyway? Rothschild? Dr Collis is, above all, determined to make me an artist, to give me a chance to realise my life's ambition, that is to provide for myself.

By the way, Dr Warnants came out to me yesterday, to ask me if I would mind painting a few pictures for his new clinic as the walls were rather bare, and of course I agreed readily. He told me they had many visitors and some might enquire who painted them. When he would tell them how they were done, someone might want to purchase them, neat little scheme what?

Sincerely,

Christy

P.S. (Thank you awfully for signing your letter 'Katriona' it is so very informal!)

Christy Brown, writing to Katriona Maguire,
January 1950

At age sixteen, Christy discovered a passionate love for classical music. As a young child he would sit and listen to the radio for hours and he eventually became fond of 'the type which the rest of the family hated and never listened to'. One day in 1948, Christy was writing upstairs in the house at Stannaway Road when he heard a piece coming from the wireless downstairs that he described as 'slow, majestic, noble . . . almost intolerably lovely'. He got off the bed where he often wrote, manoeuvred himself down the stairs, and crawled into the kitchen. As he listened, he went into a sort of trance as the music made his 'whole soul quiver with a kind of ecstasy'. When it stopped, the title of the piece was announced: Handel's 'Largo'. Music was a new world for Christy. He became addicted to listening to the great composers on the wireless as often as he could. As he listened, he would dream of going to an opera or a symphony concert. Chopin was his favourite composer; he thought he could sit and listen to his piano music for entire days. Listening to music, he said in *My Left Foot*, he felt 'an undercurrent of emotion that made me calm and hopeful, that brought with it a vague promise or message of something to come'. As he grew older, he became entranced by opera and would sit for hours, rapt, listening to broadcasts of orchestral concerts or operas. His mother would roll her eyes and say, 'You and your mad music!' Christy's younger brother Seán remembers how he would often sit listening to music, singing to himself, his left foot swinging in the air as though he were conducting an orchestra.

In 1948, music was his only release; home felt to him like 'a prison'. Christy was tired of trying to be optimistic; he started to dread getting out of bed every day. When he thought of God, it was with 'a sense of resentment'. He prayed every night with his brothers and sisters but only in an automatic way; there was no thought or sincerity behind his prayers. He began to feel that his disability was simply a senseless and terrible twist of fate he had to just deal with.

These bouts of depression would recur throughout his life. Bridget, as always, kept a close eye on Christy and she saw that he was losing his sense of hope. So she was happy when one afternoon Katriona arrived at the family home and posed the question to Christy, 'Well, what about going to Lourdes?' Bridget believed the invitation was truly God-sent.

All his life, Christy had heard people discuss this famous town of Catholic pilgrimage, where Bernadette Soubirous had a series of visions of the Virgin Mary in 1858. He told Katriona he very much wanted to go. His interest was not so much in finding God. Rather, he wanted to meet new people and see another country. This was a chance for him to break free. Christy needed stimulation; his mind would get bored sitting alone in Kimmage working from copybooks and reproducing paintings from picture books and newspapers. He dared not tell anyone but he was also excited about the idea of a miracle occurring. His mother, who had been down to the local shops, arrived in after Katriona and was thrilled at the prospect of Christy going to such a holy place. One sentiment was always expressed by Bridget to her family and friends: 'It is better to light a candle than to curse the darkness.' Her optimism never failed her.

The total cost of the trip was £34. The three of them began to make plans. The local Lourdes Committee was organising the trip and donated £10 for each person making the pilgrimage. The day after the invitation was made, Bridget asked her sister-in-law for another £5, which was as much as the family could afford to contribute. Katriona told Christy she would 'invite round all my friends and make them play bridge for something tremendous, like five shillings a hundred, and see that they all lose'. She made up the rest of the money.

Christy was nervous before he left. It was his first trip away from home, and nobody he knew would be travelling with him. He wondered if people would understand him and how he would eat. At sixteen years old, he was unable to feed, dress or wash himself – his father always did these things for him. Christy, Bridget and Patrick went to Dublin airport at three in the morning and were met by two ambulancemen, who put Christy onto a stretcher to get him on the plane. He was given a seat next to the window and his fear turned to excitement as the plane went up over the Irish Sea, above the Welsh coast and eventually across the English Channel.

Next to Christy was a girl a little older than him with long red hair, whose legs and spine were paralysed. She talked to him about books and her home in County Wicklow. Later, he 'heard her sigh wearily and pass a hand across her forehead as if in a gesture of pain. "Please God," she said, "I'll walk again some day. And *then* I'll go to my first dance." She died at Lourdes two days later.' Another young boy on the plane, whom Christy described as 'cheerful, with a pleasant voice', had no arms or legs. Directly behind him was a tubercular young woman who had contracted the disease after giving birth a year before. She fell into a coma and died in Lourdes, just days before the group was to travel back to Dublin.

When they arrived in France, volunteers helped passengers off the plane and into an open-air ambulance. They were driven to a convent, in the town of Lourdes, in the Hautes-Pyrénées, where they would stay for their seven-day pilgrimage. On the way, they passed the enormous basilica in Rosary Square, filled with crowds of people kneeling in prayer, sitting in the sunshine or walking around taking pictures. Christy and the group arrived at the convent, where they were shown their beds and given lunch. Christy was too hungry to be embarrassed at having to be fed with a spoon by a stranger. The organisers told them they should rest after the journey and that they would be taken to the famous healing baths the next day.

That night, Christy pined for home and felt scared but one of the nurses, a young woman from Dublin whom he had nicknamed 'Cherry Ripe' when he was on the plane, spotted him and saw the anxiety in his eyes. She came to his bed, smiling, and tucked him in. 'Comfy now?' she asked. 'Very,' he said. After that, he slept soundly.

In the morning, they were all taken to the healing baths, where some three hundred people were converged; about three-quarters of them were, like Christy, in wheelchairs. Two men took him by the arms and carried him into the water. They plunged him under twice and then lifted him out, afterwards offering him a cross to kiss. He was then taken to the Grotto of Massabielle, where Bernadette is said to have experienced her visions, to pray at the altar under the marble image of the Virgin Mary. Christy prayed fervently, asking that he might be cured. That evening, he went to the grotto again, for a prayer service, and he asked God over and over if he would come and cure him. Instead of a change in his body occurring that night in Lourdes, there was a change in his mind.

When Christy returned home, he remembered feeling amazed and grateful for his life. He wrote in *My Left Foot*:

> [some] of them were in wheelchairs like myself . . . Others were deprived of whole limbs, while a number went about on crutches, hobbling from place to place with difficulty. I saw them all – legless, armless, sightless, some looking like living corpses as they lay under the newly risen sun. It was like the Court of Miracles in Victor Hugo's novel. Among them I felt very small and insignificant.

Bridget had been sure before the trip that some kind of miracle would occur and in a way it had. Christy had come back with a new vision and although it was not a miraculous or religious one, he had been irrevocably changed. After his week in Lourdes, he recognised that some people were suffering even more than him. This feeling stayed with him but as he sank back into the patterns of normal family life in Kimmage, the people around him did not remind him of how lucky he was; rather, their health underlined how different he was. In Dublin he 'was surrounded not by a great multitude of the afflicted, but by my family, strong, healthy, normal individuals who, though unconsciously, made me feel rather like a puppet in contrast. Like a bird that had been set free for a while I felt as if I was about to be locked in my cage.' He would read no author but Dickens; his sad stories with often abandoned or orphaned characters suited his mood.

Only a week after coming home, he sat sadly staring out of the window in the room where he and all his brothers slept. He noticed a car light glinting through the glass, and watched as a man stopped a car, got out and checked the number on the front of their house. He then opened the front gate, and walked to the front door. That man was Dr Robert Collis.

Collis had seen Christy when he was a child on the outing to the cinema with Marrowbone Lane. He was struck by the boy's 'cherubic face', as he later wrote in his autobiography *To Be a Pilgrim*. What he did not know then was that he would meet the child again, when he was a man, and that the meeting would help to create the first treatment centre for cerebral palsy in Ireland. Collis wrote that the first time he saw Christy Brown determined him to begin researching cerebral palsy. In his autobiography, he wrote:

> One day the subject was suddenly brought to notice with tremendous force by a case which showed the terrific drama of a human soul imprisoned within an almost functionless or at least an abnormally functioning body, yet breaking forth and overcoming insurmountable difficulties. In this instance it was a boy called Christy.

Robert Collis was born in 1900 to a wealthy Anglo-Irish family. He and his two brothers all attended Rugby School. In 1918, Robert tried to join a cadet battalion outside London to train for the Irish Guards but the Great War ended so instead, in 1919, he went to Trinity College, Cambridge, to study medicine. He won a year's exchange scholarship to study at Yale University and while there he took classes in literature and poetry, developing an aspiration to become a professional writer. After graduating from Cambridge, Collis went to King's College Hospital in London. There, he studied under the famous paediatrician Sir Frederick Still and decided to specialise in child medicine. A talented sportsman, Collis played rugby while in London and a friend and fellow rugby player, Bethel Solomons, Master of the Rotunda maternity hospital, arranged for him to try out for the Irish national team. Collis succeeded and was capped against France in 1924. Solomons also suggested that Collis come and work at the Rotunda Hospital in Dublin. His internship at the Rotunda was the beginning of his interest in helping Dublin's impoverished inner city. When his internship finished, he went to America and gained experience at Johns Hopkins Hospital in Baltimore before moving to Great Ormond Street Hospital in London. Finally, he returned to Dublin to work at the Rotunda again. He was appointed a paediatrician at the hospital in 1932, the year of Christy's Brown birth.

Collis was appalled by the poor standard of care in Dublin. After working with some of the best-educated doctors in the best departments in the world, he was determined to implement the methods he saw used in Britain and the United States. His experiences in those countries were at the root of his realisation that social workers, then practically non-existent in Ireland, were crucial to creating a better health-care system.

After working to create new programmes to help update the Rotunda's paediatric health-care system, Collis still felt perturbed by children suffering from cerebral palsy who came to him for treatment. He had no experience of dealing with the illness (although he knew that ideas and procedures for easing its symptoms were being developed in other countries), so he was forced to hand anyone with cerebral palsy over to the physiotherapy departments. Collis was reasonably familiar with the condition, as his sister-in-law, Eirene Collis, had worked at Johns Hopkins under a Dr Phelps, who treated cases of cerebral palsy. On her return from America, she set up one of the first treatment centres for children with cerebral palsy, at Queen Mary's Hospital in Carshalton, a dormitory suburb south of London. When she visited her brother-in-law in Dublin, she encouraged him to set up a similar centre.

On the night he first visited the Browns, Dr Collis introduced himself to Bridget and Patrick and then walked into the front room and said hello to Christy, who had come downstairs. He told him he had seen him before and that for some reason he had stuck in his mind. Then he grew silent, paced for a few moments and told Christy for the first time what illness he suffered from and that there was help for him. 'Christy,' he said, 'there is a new treatment for cerebral palsy – the thing that is wrong with you. I believe you can be cured – but only if you are willing to try hard enough with us. I can't help you if you don't try to help yourself. You must *want* to get better before anything can be done for you.' Dr Collis leaned towards Christy and looked into his eyes. 'Will you try if I help?' Christy could not answer. Dr Collis saw the look on his face and seemed pleased. He put his arm around Christy's shoulders and announced that they would start treatment the next day. This was, for Christy, 'a miracle', because it gave him hope, when all he was feeling was 'bitterness and disillusion'.

Dr Collis also had an extraordinary effect on another writer who came from Kimmage: Brendan Behan. As Behan's biographer, the writer and playwright Ulick O'Connor, remembers, 'When Brendan was in borstal and he was seventeen or eighteen, he read this book, *The Silver Fleece* by Bob Collis . . . it gave him an identity with Ireland which he badly needed at that time, jailed in England during the war as the little Irish boy. Brendan used to see himself, he says in *Borstal Boy*, running down the field, playing rugby for Ireland, and all this was inspired by this great book. So that had a very big influence on Brendan and when he came back to Dublin, he got to meet Collis.

'It was funny because one is a slum boy and the other was from the only real, what should I call it, "Brahmin class", the medical profession and the lawyers. Because, you see, the landed gentry really didn't run Dublin society. It was run by Dublin Castle and the lawyers and the doctors.'

Dr Louis Warnants, one of Collis's colleagues, arrived at the Brown household the day after Collis's visit to begin a routine of physiotherapy with Christy. Dr Warnants was tall, with a solid build and a similar character. He came to see Christy every Sunday from that first day and they would go through simple exercises of stretching and moving Christy's limbs in an attempt to get them more relaxed and to help build up his muscles. Often when Dr Warnants arrived, the house was too crowded for them to do the exercises properly, so Warnants would firmly suggest to Christy's brothers and sisters that it was a nice day for a walk and point them towards the door. The only room he and Christy could work in was the kitchen and Christy would often end up with his legs hitting the fire-grate or, as he lay on his stomach stretching out his arms and legs, his head would smack against the furniture. The problem was a lack of room and as Bridget watched the two struggling to do their best in such a confined space, an idea formed in her mind.

For years, the small patch of land at the back of the house had been unused. Bridget would often offer money to the children if they would do something with it and they had tried to use it to grow turnips and other vegetables but the soil never seemed to allow anything to grow. So Bridget decided to build a room there for Christy. She carefully made enquiries of all her bricklayer sons as to the cost of materials for such a project, without ever letting anyone know what she was planning. After a few weeks, she estimated that the cost of building the room from scratch would be £50. She began selling things and borrowing and saving bits of money when she could. She joined money clubs (a system whereby a housewife could make payments to an agent to allow purchase of goods on credit or to accumulate savings), took whatever she could to the pawnshop and looked up old relatives who she thought might be kind enough to make a small contribution. Christy's younger brother Eamonn (the ninth child in the family) remembers they often ate 'blind stew' in those days – so called because there was nothing in it.

When Bridget had managed to get £20 put together, she decided to make a start. Her sons all said they would be happy to help but no one rolled up his sleeves and started the project; it seemed they were all waiting for someone else to show the initiative. So Bridget took it upon herself to get a room built for Christy: 'She went out one afternoon and ordered a hundred concrete blocks, four bags of cement and two bags of mortar.' That night when Patrick arrived home, he was aghast. What, he asked her, did she think she was doing? She was building a room for Christy, she told him. He was worried they might all be evicted. Dublin Corporation did not allow any of the houses that their tenants lived in to have extensions. Bridget replied, 'Yes, yes, I know all that. But do take your dinner now, like a good man, or it'll be cold on you.'

'Only over my dead body,' said Patrick.

'I'd bury your body first, of course,' she replied.

Patrick said that he would not help and his sons were told not to lift a finger either. Bridget smiled and said, 'Very well, if none of you will do it, I'll build it myself.' Everyone laughed at this; it was unthinkable that she would or could do such a thing.

The next day, Bridget woke early, got breakfast ready quickly, sent the children off to school and finished her housework before lunch. She spent the afternoon in the garden, on her knees, laying out a line of blocks. When the family came in, she served everyone dinner, cleaned up and then quietly went back to her work in the back yard. Patrick went outside and stared at what she had done.

'What's this? What do you think you're doing?' he asked.

'I'm building Christy's house,' she told him, adding another block to the wall she had started. Patrick examined the wall, raised an eyebrow and said, 'You're doing it all wrong, woman. Where's your foundation?'

He called his sons to take a look at the work. They agreed it was a mess.

'Well, if it's a man's job,' she said, 'get on with it.'

Christy watched the whole scenario and as his mother walked away from the small wall she had built, she smiled at him.

Patrick and his sons worked on the room for weeks. One day, when it was half-finished – with only the four walls and the foundation in place – Patrick asked Christy what he thought. 'Like an unfinished symphony,' Christy answered.

After a few months, the work was done. The room was originally intended to be like a small gymnasium, where Dr Warnants and Christy could work together out of the way of the family. But Christy began to paint, read, write, eat and sleep in what would from then on be referred to by everyone in the house, including himself, as his 'study'.

The treatment Christy received from Dr Warnants was only the start of his rehabilitation. Dr Collis called in to him only a few weeks after his study had been built and told him that he wanted him to go to England to be seen by his sister-in-law, Eirene Collis. He wanted her to determine whether Christy was a good candidate to enter a full-time course of treatment for cerebral palsy. Christy felt that everything in his future now rested on Eirene Collis's decision.

Warnants, Bridget and Christy left Dublin for London on a Saturday morning in 1949 to meet Eirene Collis at the Middlesex Hospital. The three waited for her in a small office. When she walked in, she was holding a cigarette. She said hello, introduced herself and smoked calmly. She asked Christy how old he was and when Bridget went to answer for him, she held up her hand and said that she'd like Christy to answer himself. He told her his age; normally he would not have been understood, but Eirene Collis did understand him. She told him she thought he had been a cripple long enough. Christy smiled and decided that he trusted her. An assistant then came in and Christy was stripped and gently hoisted onto a table to be examined. He writes that he was very scared, but he refused to say anything. Being examined by doctors was something he had been through many times and although he knew that Eirene Collis and Louis Warnants respected and understood him, memories came back of all the times he had been seen by doctors before. Many years later, in his novel *Down All the Days*, he would write of his visits to hospitals in Dublin:

> 'I won't hurt you, dear,' said the nurse in a whisper . . . every muscle and nerve coiled taut as a spring, as she went about her task, inserting the soft rubber tube down his delicate passage, moving quietly, competently, as if it were an ordinary thing like knitting or stringing beads; he felt defenceless, outraged, ashamed, and conscious of a quick yet muffled pain as the tube sank deeper into him . . .
>
> A nurse came in and began to feed him with hot milk . . . it was not the same one who had performed such a strange service for him last night, and he was glad, for he could not have met her eyes . . . he lay in a strange room, in a cool bed, marooned; and suddenly the sheets securely roped in under the mattress became his chains, soft linen chains holding him down. He remembered a sparrow lying writhing in the front garden, maimed by a shot from his brother's catapult, its wing shattered, squawking wildly; at first he had laughed with the rest, seeing it hobbling about with frantic futility, trying to fly, to regain its own element again, its own small dignity; then he had felt slightly sick and was glad when someone got a stone and put the wrecked, crippled thing out of its misery.

The day Christy saw the bird with the broken wing always stayed with him. He would use the image many times in his poetry and the above passage shows how vulnerable and frightened he was when he thought of doctors and medical care. As Eirene Collis examined him, no doubt he was terrified of being too hopeful. The news was good and bad. Eirene said he could be 'cured' but in order to achieve this, he must agree to use his left foot no longer. She insisted that he must not use his foot for anything – eating, painting or writing. She told him that a special chair must be built for him to sit in that would improve his posture; he would have to be strapped into it as much as possible. His family would christen it 'the electric chair'.

Although Eirene Collis believed that Christy's use of his foot had been of great value in that it had allowed him to express himself, she thought that the rest of his body was suffering because he was constantly concentrating on using his left foot. Since he controlled this foot with such extraordinary dexterity, the rest of his body had been left to run wild.

Christy was upset – his foot was his independence. But he saw the logic of the argument and agreed to commit to stopping using his left foot. When he came back to Kimmage, he wrote to Katriona:

> I am writing this letter with a mixed feeling of regret and determination: regret as this is the last letter I shall write for the next five years: determined to write the next letter with my hands. Am I mad you wonder? The answer is no. I flew to London with my mother yesterday (Saturday) morning with a feeling of curiosity and expectancy: last night I arrived in Dublin with a feeling of hope and determination in my heart . . . please God the next time I pick up a paint brush it will be with my hand, between my fingers, not between my toes, then I'll paint your portrait! I will walk up to the door of 'Garvagh' and we will celebrate with me and my gal!

. . . who knows what the dim and distant future may hold? If determination and grit has a say it holds happiness, prosperity, independence and good living, as far as our correspondence is concerned it is au revoir, but as to our friendship – that is endless! Impregnable! Goodbye until you next read at the bottom of a page –
Yours (very) sincerely,
Christy.

P.S. (I have painted my last picture with my feet. It is on glass and I have done it especially for your little boy.)

Dr Robert Collis met Christy off the plane from London and told him he had heard the wonderful news. He also told him he had managed to form a cerebral palsy clinic, using a gymnasium at the back of the Orthopaedic Hospital in Merrion Street, Dublin. The Knights of Malta and the St John Ambulance Brigade had agreed to provide transport for Dublin patients to attend classes from nine in the morning to midday. Christy told Collis he wanted to attend and so was taken for his first therapy session the next Monday morning.

When he arrived at the clinic, he was appalled. As the doors of the gymnasium opened, a horrific din filled his ears, children howling and screaming, the sounds echoing back off the walls. Dr Warnants took Christy inside and as they entered the room, Christy wrote, 'the full force of the noise hit me with an almost physical sensation'. He looked around him and saw that there was no person there of his own age. Most of the patients were young children, under twelve years of age. Christy felt that he was trapped in a bizarre nightmare. This was much worse than the suffering in Lourdes. There, the adults had had terrible afflictions but they were capable of understanding their illness or at least resigning themselves to it. Here, there was no sense or reason. He saw 'helplessness and near-horror in the form of twisting, twining babies with crooked little limbs, misshapen heads, distorted features', and he suddenly realised what he himself had looked like when he was an infant.

Christy gazed at the children with pity and then stopped himself, remembering how he hated pity. During his first weeks at the clinic, he asked himself why he was there. He felt he did not belong. Still, doctors' letters and reports from the time do not mention Christy displaying a negative attitude towards the clinic. Instead, they often say how encouraging he was to the children around him and how kind words from him frequently made all the difference to those small children. Both the staff and the students at the Cerebral Palsy Clinic saw Christy Brown as a leader. When Collis took a £100 donation from the Marrowbone Lane Fund to establish a clinic that was held in the afternoons at the Children's Hospital in Harcourt Street (later moving to Bull Alley Street), he did not realise that this was the genesis of the only group that would provide care and information for sufferers of the condition in Ireland: Cerebral Palsy Ireland (now called Enable Ireland). By 1951, Collis would establish Cerebral Palsy Ireland as a national association, gathering together subscribers and directors from the Rotunda Hospital and the Marrowbone Lane Fund and appointing them as directors. Ulick O'Connor knew Christy, Bridget and Dr Collis well and he says: 'His mother is the real key but after that it's the actual trainers [Robert and Eirene Collis], these two people who provided a facility without which Christy couldn't have done anything, really. He would have survived, she [Bridget] was there for him, but he couldn't have become a world figure, I think, without them.'

Mona, Christy's elder sister, agreed, saying: 'Cerebral palsy wasn't known about then, you know. It was twenty years before they realised it was cerebral palsy. You know, nobody knew anything about this until Christy's story came out. He wasn't the first but he was the first to be discovered.'

Chapter Six

A BOOK

I suppose you have observed by now my obvious hesitance to enter into any lengthy conversations with anyone, sometimes not even with my family, my main verbal output being short monosyllables such as 'yes' or 'no'. But even if I did not express my gratitude in words, I felt it all the more and besides I am convinced that it would be practically impossible for me to convey my immense thanks to you . . . in mere human words . . .

Your numerous kindnesses to me are indeed past forgetting. I am afraid I shall never be the friend to you that you have been to me. That would be an impossibility for many reasons.

But the long broad vista of the future is spread out before me and who can tell what an adventurer like me will discover? It may be heartening success or dismal failure. But I am determined to find out which it will be. The book [*My Left Foot*] is progressing along the appropriate lines and is steadily increasing in volume. I have already completed four chapters and intend beginning the fifth immediately, when this letter is finished. I do not often ask the boon of prayers but please do offer one now and again for the success of this book. I am putting heart and soul into it. I intend writing twelve chapters which will take about two years to complete.

Certainly, it is strenuous work, but I revel in it and my reward will be its success. If it is a success then I definitely intend taking up a literary career. I think my theme will be

essays. A subject that I am not particularly deplorable at. Of course, my lack of proper education will be a disadvantage, but I do not consider it insurmountable. Certainly I shall not be baulked by it. One does not have to be an Oxford 'don' to write a book. Further, I am of the opinion that one does not have to necessarily possess a college education in order to gain a niche in the literary world. Still, I often wonder if I shall ever see my book in print . . . what do you think about the transmigration of souls? It would be great if I had the soul of Carlyle or Ruskin. What a hope that is!
 Christy

Christy Brown, writing to Katriona Maguire,
1950

Christy began working on his memoir, *My Left Foot*, in 1950, while he was attending the Cerebral Palsy Clinic. He was reflective, contemplating his fate as a disabled man. He had 'some inner urge to speak' and he knew he wanted to express himself to a larger audience. He felt that in discovering the desire to tell his story, he had found a way of 'playing my part in the world of the able-bodied'. But he was flummoxed as to how he could express himself to the public: 'My hands were of no use to me at all . . . Nor could my lips utter the thoughts which were whirling round in my mind like swarms of impatient bees, because I still wasn't able to speak any sort of intelligible language outside the family circle.' Nor could he use his left foot; that would be a betrayal of Eirene Collis. After days of wondering what he should do, Christy had an idea as he watched his younger brother Eamonn struggling with a composition for school. Just as he had done with his brother Paddy for the paints, he offered Eamonn a swap: he told him that he would help him write the essay if Eamonn would do something for him in return.

'Sure I will,' Eamonn replied. 'What do you want me to do?'

'Write my life story,' Christy told him.

The pair started working together in Christy's study, with Eamonn taking dictation every day. Christy's writing was always a compulsion: he needed to tell his story and he was desperate to communicate with the outside world. He was still reading Dickens and so his prose was written in stolid Victorian language. After filling four hundred pages of old school jotters in an attempt to make a first draft of the book, Eamonn was exhausted and Christy was frustrated. He became bad-tempered and took his frustration out on Eamonn at first, then the rest of the family. The brothers kept working, but as the book (then entitled 'The Reminiscences of a Mental Defective') dragged on, Christy grew more and more angry. He struggled for more than a year and a half and for all that time he was unable to express one thought in one simple sentence. He wrote, 'I required three or four sentences before being satisfied I'd expressed my meaning, and sometimes I would use up a whole paragraph to express a single thought.' He found himself lost in 'a forest of words' and became violent, using his left foot to kick aside anything that got in his way.

Christy knew that he needed advice. At first, he could not think of anyone who could help him but, on reflection, the answer occurred to him. He yelled for Eamonn and told him to write on a postcard: 'I'm trying to write a book. If you don't mind, please come and help me. Christy Brown.' Then he instructed Eamonn to send the message to Doctor Robert Collis straight away. Christy did not know until later that Collis had written the plays *Marrowbone Lane* (1939) and *The Barrel Organ* (1940), both produced and directed by Hilton Edwards and Micheál Mac Liammóir, and an autobiography, *The Silver Fleece* (1936). Nor did he know that both Collis's brothers were authors (John Stewart and Maurice Collis) or that Collis's friends included Seán O'Faoláin (a famous Irish short-story writer), Frank O'Connor, Cecil Day-Lewis (the British Poet Laureate from 1968 to 1972) and Lord Longford.

Collis arrived the next day and read the manuscript there and then. After trawling through the pages, he found a sentence that was good and which showed him that Christy had the potential to write well. Collis said this to Christy. He also told him that he had to make serious changes to his style and the language. For Collis, a writer had to 'have a story to tell' and be able to 'tell it in a way that the person reading it can live in it himself'. Collis then lent him books by L.A.G. Strong and O'Faoláin. Thus Christy began his second draft of *My Left Foot.*

Another person who was to play a major part in Christy's development as a writer was Dr Patricia Sheehan. They met on 8 October 1952, at the National Association for Cerebral Palsy day centre in Bull Alley Street in Dublin (known with fondness by those who worked there as 'the Auld Beano'). Dr Sheehan had come to the clinic as a volunteer speech therapist. Christy was delighted to meet her; his speech was the one thing he most wanted to improve and he was highly motivated.

He had severe dysarthria (disordered or impaired articulation of speech caused by disturbances in muscle control, usually resulting from damage to the central or peripheral nervous system). His jaw jerked to one side and sometimes even locked itself. Christy and Dr Sheehan's friendship grew through many hours of hard work together and eventually she could understand his speech. She was struck by his quick wit, humour and magnetic personality. In her notes, now held in the National Library of Ireland, she wrote:

> Within a few minutes of conversing with him, one completely forgot his physical handicap, you were so busily engrossed in communicating with him. He was a very keen observer, he grinned and called you an 'eejit' if you didn't quite get the meaning of what he was saying and then heaved a sigh when you did.

In March 1953, the clinic moved again, from Bull Alley Street to St Brendan's Hospital in Sandymount Avenue, on the south side of Dublin. Christy attended physiotherapy and speech therapy and worked long hours with Dr Sheehan, trying to relax his jaw and facial muscles and to control his breathing.

One afternoon, while Christy and Dr Sheehan were working together during a session, she introduced him to a new patient called Bernard. Bernard was from Belfast, a residential patient at the clinic and a protégé of Dr Collis. He was unable to speak intelligibly, so he used a spelling board. Bernard and Christy immediately disliked one another. Bernard complained that he was unable to understand Christy owing to his impaired speech, while Christy found it impossible to follow Bernard's flashing fingers spelling out words. Like children, they both fought for Dr Sheehan's attention, each believing she belonged exclusively to him. After the meeting, Christy commented, 'That poor fella stuck in there in a clinical setting – he can't even get out for an auld jar.' For his part, Bernard's resentment of Christy did not recede and he later attacked the adorned quality of Christy's style, spelling out on his board to Dr Sheehan, 'You can see the effects of overcrowding even in Christy's writing.'

Speech therapy was scary for Christy; the term itself intimidated him. But he was struck by the straightforward nature of the exercises. He wrote in *My Left Foot*: 'its methods were so simple that I felt anyone could have thought them out'. He worked with Dr Sheehan, at first simply blowing bubbles; then, by using a straw, he had to push water from one bottle to another connected to it. His breathing, like the rest of the movements of his body, was jerky and spasmodic and he had to work on controlling his inhalations and exhalations before he could learn to speak more clearly. He thought that his speech problem really came not from his muscle spasms but from fear. Breath-control exercises helped him, but shame welled up inside him whenever he tried to converse with anyone. His skin would burn as the blood rose to his neck and his tension often stopped him enunciating words clearly. Even when Collis would come to the family house to discuss his work, Christy became 'awkward and embarrassed . . . and felt [his] face growing red'. So Christy listened as Collis talked and taught him as much as he could about writing.

Christy continued working on *My Left Foot* throughout 1953, with his thirteen-year-old brother Francis replacing Eamonn as his scribe. As the process went on, Bridget insisted that each child should go out to Christy in his study and transcribe for him. Each day after school, she would send one of the younger children to take notes for him or help him with his work. As his younger sister Ann remembers, 'I mean, I was only ten or eleven and he was giving us these big words. He would make you do it six or seven times until you'd got it right and maybe two days later you'd come across that particular word again and he'd say, "I told you that the other day, you should remember it." I can honestly say I turned out the best speller. I mightn't understand the words but I can spell anything, because you were kicked in the shins with his left foot if you didn't remember. He was like a teacher. And I would often come in crying, saying "Ah, I don't want to go out today! He gives me a kick if I can't spell! He's after kicking my shins!"'

Together, Francis and Christy finished a second draft, which was more succinct in terms of its themes and its language. But Collis told Christy that it was full of clichés and that the prose sometimes rambled incoherently for pages. Christy did not know what a cliché was. No one had ever explained this to him. Collis advised Christy to start a new draft and agreed to find a private tutor for him. Collis and Katriona discussed the idea and decided that between them they might find someone suitable. Through the help of the local church and the parish priest, Father Mullane, they found a master in one of the large schools in Kimmage who said he would love to teach Christy and would come to Stannaway Road to meet him. His name was Mr Guthrie, a middle-aged, good-humoured man.

Slowly and steadily, they surmounted the barrier of the young man's speech, although Christy most often simply listened. He would respond to straightforward questions by saying yes or no but for more difficult questions Mr Guthrie had to be patient with his student, while Christy faced his fear of being embarrassed by his own speech. This was always a key fact in Christy's life: certain people could understand him if they took the time and made the effort to do so. When someone did that, Christy would trust them and let down his barriers. Guthrie and Christy became so comfortable with one another that, after formal teaching sessions, they would sit and discuss subjects as varied as Bertrand Russell, the poetry of Yeats and psychoanalysis. Christy was interested in geometry but otherwise hated mathematics (so much so that he would sometimes get his younger brother Seán to do his homework for him). But for some reason, angles, triangles and theorems fascinated him. He also loved Latin but reading a new novel or play was what really thrilled him.

He beavered away at his third draft of *My Left Foot*. Although the education he was getting was a great source of happiness for him, his emotions were not stable. The realisation of his own strangeness continued to sadden him. He watched as his older brothers went out to work and were meeting girls and having fun. He felt caged. One night, Christy called Francis in to work on the new draft of *My Left Foot* but he could think of nothing to say. The words were all there, waiting to be said, but he could not find the way to say them. He stared at his hands; they were 'useless as ever'. Then he remembered his left foot. He told Francis to 'get the hell out' of his study. Alone, he pulled off his shoe, put a pencil between his toes and wrote the final draft of his first book. He wrote for days without stopping and he was thrilled to know 'the ecstasy of creating'.

Collis read the first chapter of *My Left Foot* and told Christy that he was on to a winner. He said that he would send the work to his agent and use some of his literary connections to see what kind of publishing deal could be made. Collis was so impressed with Christy's work that he asked him if he might allow him to read the first chapter at a fund-raising evening for cerebral palsy. The clinic was still in need of money and Collis was planning an event to increase publicity for the Marrowbone Lane Fund. In the aftermath of the Second World War, he had worked as a volunteer in hospitals in mainland Europe, helping sick children and survivors of the Belsen concentration camp. While in Germany, he met two orphaned children and he brought them back to Dublin with him. One of the children, Zoltan, suffered from tuberculosis of the spine and had had the major part of his left lung removed. Collis often took him to Brompton Chest Hospital in England for care. While on one of these visits, he happened to meet his acquaintance Burl Ives (a popular folk and country singer who also starred in several films), who was working as a volunteer entertainer in the children's ward. Collis asked him if he would be so good as to assist him with his work on cerebral palsy in Ireland and Ives agreed immediately to help him raise funds.

The benefit took place in the Aberdeen Hall of the Gresham Hotel in Dublin's city centre and was sponsored by the Ireland America Society. The event was widely publicised in the press and more than five hundred tickets were sold; people ended up standing at the sides of the room. Christy was on stage with Dr Collis and the film director John Huston (then president of the Ireland America Society). Burl Ives opened the show and received a raucous welcome. After Ives' performance, Huston introduced Collis, who rose to address the audience: 'I'm not going to make a speech. I'm not even going to make an appeal. I'm just going to read you something that will give you an inside view of a person crippled with cerebral palsy. The first chapter of Christy Brown's autobiography here' – he extended his arm to Christy – 'written with his left foot.'

As Collis read Christy's work, everyone in the room fell silent. Christy was astounded when he realised how intently the audience was listening. He stared at the crowd and felt his body relax more profoundly than it had ever done before. When Collis stopped reading, the audience remained silent. Christy noticed a young girl weeping in the front row. He looked at his mother and saw that her eyes too were filling with tears despite her efforts to hold them back. His own father seemed to look at him in a new way. Collis walked over to Christy and helped him to stand and the crowd began cheering. A man appeared on stage with a bunch of red roses, which Collis took over to Bridget. Christy's brothers and sisters were 'cheering and yelling like hell'. For the first time since he had realised he was different to others, when he was only a young child, Christy felt 'at peace'.

Collis made all the necessary contacts for Christy through his agent and author friends, and the publishers Secker & Warburg in London agreed to bring the book out, as did Simon & Schuster in America. *My Left Foot*'s acceptance for publication in 1954 was celebrated at Collis's house at 26 Fitzwilliam Square, with singing and drinking going on until the late hours. Collis wrote a foreword and an epilogue for the book (which are in print only in the first edition). The foreword reads, in part:

> Many years ago . . . I saw a strange looking little boy perched on the shoulders of a bigger and much stronger boy. They presented a most amazing spectacle so that I can still see the picture clearly. The horse was broad-shouldered, had dark tousled hair and his lips were twisted in a funny smile of confidence, strength and friendliness. The rider's legs were twisted round him, his arms and hands held stiff in an odd way. What has remained most clearly in my mind, however, was the pale young face and the eyes that seemed to shine with vitality from it. The photograph . . . where Christy is

depicted painting with his left foot will give the reader the best visual picture of what I saw at that moment. Indeed, though he is now a man of twenty-two, I can still see the same rare spiritual quality in his gaze.

That look in his eyes that Collis saw is something almost everyone who met Christy Brown – including Jim Sheridan, Peter Sheridan and Richard Harris – would always remember.

Secker & Warburg gave the book a formal launch in London, at the Irish Club in Eaton Square. Dr Collis wrote in his autobiography *To Be a Pilgrim* that the evening was wonderful and wild; inebriated waiters let the wine flow, announcing that everyone should have 'another sup of the craythure [whiskey]'. The publishers' representatives loudly called for the bar to be closed. Bridget ended up sitting on Cecil-Day Lewis's or Lord Longford's lap (she could not remember which). Katriona attended, as did many of Christy's family.

For the author, it was a truly surreal occasion. The launch was a dream now turned into reality, as was the success and the money that went with it. The Dublin typewriter manufacturer J.A. Miller, of J.A. Miller & Son in Dublin, sent Christy a typewriter after Collis cleverly included in his introduction to *My Left Foot* an oblique hint that such a donation would be appreciated in the Brown household. Christy loved his new machine; it meant that he could write more quickly and clearly to more people. He christened it 'Iron Sally'.

My Left Foot first caught the attention of periodicals and magazines and was serialised in Ireland and England by *John Bull* and in America by *Good Housekeeping*, as well as in local newspapers in Dublin. It grew in popularity, and sales figures steadily increased after its release. It was translated into French, German, Italian, Dutch, Japanese and Braille. Crowds of journalists arrived at Stannaway Road to see Christy and interview him, with the help of his family working as 'translators'.

Christy's younger sister Ann remembers how even then Christy would become incensed if the interviewer spoke to his brothers and sisters about him rather than speaking directly to him. Sometimes the interviewer would not even look at him but would only make eye contact with whoever was interpreting. The Browns would joke about the reluctance of the journalists to acknowledge Christy, referring to this type of attitude as 'Does he take sugar?'

Christy would diffuse such situations by coming up with a quip or a shocking statement, as if to say, *I am here. I am an artist. I will not be ignored.* As his sister Ann says, 'What I used to see was, during the interviews he would give – 'cause I used to have to interpret for him – I felt an awful lot of people would talk above him instead of at him. It was as if because he had a physical disability, that meant he had a mental disability. And I would say, "Talk to him as Christy." He was frustrated with that, because he was so intense and intelligent that he couldn't understand [a journalist] talking to me and not him. That used to frustrate him and he'd be cursing and mumbling but of course they couldn't understand him and we would laugh afterwards, because I would be covering up for him, do you know what I mean? I was thinking that language-wise . . . I mean, he could speak to you and I know eventually the speech therapist helped him a bit but 'twas never like yourself or myself, so, you see, in a sense his language was that of someone who has never really spoken or experienced exchange but has this intense mind that has accumulated everything, and it was miraculous.'

Ann also has happy memories of Christy and interviews. She was with him once when an American film crew came to do an interview with him and he was suffering from a terrible hangover, so when the crew arrived, Ann had to try to think of a reason for his not being ready. She couldn't be bothered to come up with an excuse, so she just told them they would have to wait, he'd had a few jars the night before and wasn't even up yet. When Christy did finally emerge, the film crew rose to their feet and applauded him – Ann couldn't believe it.

Even during the early stages of his career, Christy was never one to allow himself to be patronised or turned into a subject to be regarded with mawkish sentimentality. When the journalist James Murray, from the St Patrick's Mission Society in County Wicklow, asked him, 'Christy, do you ever wonder what you might have been if you hadn't had your terrible handicap?', Christy doubled up in his wheelchair and laughed. 'I know,' he answered, 'I know. I would have been a good bricklayer like my father.' His attitude could be summed up in the words of a heretofore unpublished poem, 'Invitation to the Trance':

> . . . so do not sit in silent rage –
> get yourself a larger cage.

On 24 August and again on 8 September 1954, a BBC crew came to Kimmage to record a radio programme about *My Left Foot*. Mrs Brown was not expecting them the first time they turned up. She later said, 'There I was, up to my oxters [armpits] in the throes of it, and there was a pile of empty stout bottles in the yard!' She threw an old mat over them and 'let on it was a stack of turf'. The BBC crew interviewed Dr Collis, Mrs Brown, Katriona Maguire, Christy and all his siblings. They paid Christy two guineas for his contribution and the hour-long show was broadcast on the Home Service on 10 October 1954.

The cheques that arrived from Christy's publisher were sent to Dr Collis, who kept Christy's money and essentially took on the role of accountant for him. Seán remembers that when Christy wanted his money, he would tell one of his brothers or sisters to cycle or walk down to Fitzwilliam Square, where a maid or butler would answer the door. The sibling would say that Christy wanted some money and wait patiently in the hall for it to be brought. Seán was overwhelmed by the beauty of the house. To him, the whole scene was 'like something out of Charles Dickens'.

Christy's life had changed drastically. He had enough money to hire taxis, go into the city and frequent all the pubs. As the media and money came into his life, so did independence and a first real love affair, with a married woman named Beth Moore, a young English teacher from Stamford, Connecticut. She began writing to Christy in 1954 after she had read *My Left Foot*. A friend had lent Beth a copy of *Good Housekeeping*, with a recommendation she try the casserole recipe. In the magazine was an excerpt from *My Left Foot*. Beth was an upper-middle-class, east-coast American Wasp, ten years older than Christy and married to a scientist called Deac. Both she and Christy were very lonely – particularly in terms of intellectual exchange. None of his close family or friends know when their letter writing moved from fan mail to friendship and on to a serious relationship. Extramarital affairs would have been frowned upon in Ireland, so Christy did not discuss the affair very often and when he did, it was with his brother Seán, many years after it had begun. For Beth, speaking to anyone about her feelings for Christy would have jeopardised her marriage and her home life. Initially, she must have sat reading that extract from *My Left Foot* and wondered at the tenacity and strength of Christy's character; presumably this is why she began writing to him. Many women wrote to Christy in a flirtatious or suggestive manner after they read his published work. For some reason, Beth captured his imagination more than any of them and he would later dedicate his greatest literary work to her.

Christy wanted love in his life more than anything, as he wrote to Katriona:

> If people such as I cannot be romantic, what the hell else can we be – anchorites? As long as we know that we are indulging in fantasies, not what is so loosely called 'real life', I do not see why a physical disability

should preclude any romance in one's life. Life is the greatest romance of all, not in an abstract way as the scientists and philosophers and anthropologists see it; but as we live it and feel it and respond to it, with our minds and hearts and senses. If I happen to be more vulnerable, more susceptible to the challenge of life and love, it is my misfortune or blessing, whichever way I meet the challenge: either way the presence of pain will be inevitable, as a stimulant or disaster. I will cherish my romantic 'fantasies' as long as I live, knowing them to be as real as anything else in life and more acceptable than the so-called 'realities' of others. Life has made me as practical as the next person, but it has never robbed me of my dreams and I am as much an idealist now as I was in the old days, hurting just as deeply even if the pain does not last very long and I am equipped mentally and emotionally to deal with it. I could no more *not* be romantic than I could learn to fly to the moon: without this romantic streak I would be duller and less original than I am. If my particular kind of artistic appreciation lies with beautiful women . . . who the hell's complaining? Dante wasn't confined to Beatrice I bet, and it is an irrefutable fact of history that behind every great poem or book or painting there is a woman or women, since these fellows were usually accustomed to pluralities.

He did not know that the first letter he received from Beth Moore was to be the beginning of the romance he had always wanted.

On 27 May 1955, in the midst of Christy's new-found success, his father died. Bridget found him late at night. She had come in from shopping and all of the children were in and asleep. She was alarmed when she heard a low wailing noise coming from the bathroom. Patrick had hit his head on the bathtub and could not get up. He was taken to hospital, where he stayed for a short while, largely incoherent, and he passed away within a matter of days. Since he had served in the 1916 Easter Rising, he was given a military burial; his coffin was covered with the Irish tricolour flag and soldiers fired shots over his grave. Christy insisted on walking to the grave, with his brothers supporting him by his elbows. When one of them suggested that they carry him, Christy threatened them, telling them to 'try it', and he continued walking. Christy's private collected papers contain recollections of his father's funeral:

'And he that believeth in Me though he die shall liveth in Me forever . . .' The flinty no-nonsense unbreakfasted voice of the priest grinded out the words over the gulf of the grave and over the ponderous bulk of the Bible held high in pudgy hairy-jointed agricultural fingers. 'For I am the Resurrection and the Life . . .' The wind caught the words and flung them about like leaves tumbling over the grass and the dust and ashes were grey and sour in the mouth of the priest and the sodden bedraggled flag fluttered forlornly around the trestled coffin, below the black jaws of the earth waiting, above mourners huddled in miserable wind-swept little clusters now in their grief-black garments finding no warmth in either words or the climbing sun.

The black tie. It was his first tie. It lay coiled around his neck like a soft silk noose or a snake curling tighter with every impatient or impetuous movement he made. It lay like a burning black scapula about his throat, the knot just under his Adam's apple gently, caressingly throttling him as that grey gaunt ghost of a day had gone on, the heaped wreaths on the hearse in front of them wrapped in cellophane glistening with rain, their carriages swaying lightly from side to side as it rolled over the wet cobblestones and rounded the endless dingy corners of the early morning city . . .

He sat between two elder brothers on the pull-out seat behind the glass partition between them and the driver, watching his mother's face from time to time under the dark lace veil, two of his sisters flanking her on each side. She was pale and intent, occasionally glancing over at him for long moments not saying anything. She held a neat black and red covered prayerbook between gloved hands, one of which she would lift to her eyes or her forehead from time to time and leave it there for a while . . . after a short time he realised they were not moving and looked over at Mother to see why they had stopped, but she was looking out the window, leaning forward, a hand resting on her daughter's knee for support, and then he saw the tears shining behind her veil. He looked out. All he saw at first was the front of a small grey public-house with drawn dark green shutters and heavy mauve curtains drawn across the front upper windows. Then he saw set into the wall over the door a small gold plaque inscribed to the memory of a blind Irish poet who had been born in the same premises and whose melancholy verses later became famous and travelled the world.

Because Patrick Brown had worked for Dublin Corporation all his life, Bridget, as his widow, was now entitled to work for them and she took a full-time job as a cleaner. In some ways, she found being alone liberating. She went to London to see Seán and told him as much. They went out into the city at night, drinking and meeting people. Bridget played the mouth organ at his local pub in Shepherd's Bush, chatting with the punters and staying until closing time. The money that Christy was earning from *My Left Foot* allowed him to take his mother out and, to a certain degree, to replace his father's role in the household. The bond between him and Bridget remained impregnable and they always had fun together. One evening, they went to the Old Theatre Royal in Hawkins Street in Dublin. When they came out, it was half past ten, and they decided they would have a drink before closing time. They went into a pub where they were not known. Christy looked inebriated, hopping on his left foot and leaning back against his mother, who was holding him up under his arms. Her purse was in Christy's pocket and when she went to pay for the drinks, the barman rang the gardaí, saying, 'There's an auld pro on the premises robbing off a drunk.'

By 1956, Christy had begun to feel that his time was too precious and he ought to be at home writing and reading rather than spending time trying to 'cure' his condition. He wrote to Dr Sheehan saying he was sorry but he wanted to leave his treatment behind altogether, telling her that 'Physiotherapy has done all it can do for me.' He wanted to forget what he could not do and focus on what he could. The money that he earned from his memoir gave him hope that a career as a full-time writer could pay the bills. On 16 March 1956, Dr Collis wrote to him and said he had 'got quite a big cheque in' and he wanted Christy to endorse it so that they could get it through to him 'straight away on account of income tax'. Collis also opened a special investment account for Christy. This, so the doctor hoped, would leave Christy with a small, low-interest account, from which he would withdraw only what he needed, providing him with some level of financial security.

In February, Christy had had another success as a professional writer, publishing a short story, 'Sally', in the national *Evening Press*. In the story, an invalid in a wheelchair watches a woman called Sally go by his window every day. He writes her a letter and, through his writing, manages to win her over and get his first date. The story was undoubtedly inspired by his blossoming romance with Beth Moore. Like the narrator, Johnny, he felt a new confidence in his writing and in himself. Johnny watches the woman he is infatuated with from his window until he gathers the courage inside himself to contact her through letters. Just as Christy had envisioned in his mind a real, tangible relationship with a woman coming into his life, so does Johnny. As Christy and Beth became more honest and personal about their feelings towards one another, his fear that a woman would write to him and then lose interest and cease writing, or indeed (as would happen later in his life) see him in the flesh and be unable to cope with his disability, grew. For Beth, his disability was far less important than his romantic words, great sense of humour and ardent love for her. Never, in the twelve years during which they wrote and then met and made love on more than one occasion, did she falter in loving him. In one instance, she cut off a lock of her hair and enclosed it in a letter to Kimmage. She told him of the dreary, long and lonely days she had spent with her husband, playing with the curl she had sent to him, thinking of being in his arms.

As for Dr Sheehan, in response to Christy's letter telling her that he was leaving the clinic, she decided to continue their friendship and she began visiting him at home, as she also wanted him to keep up with his speech therapy. Sheehan's notes record how much Christy enjoyed listening to his own poetry being read out to him. Nearly all writers read their work out loud to themselves but this was something Christy could never do. He asked Sheehan if she would record a poem on which he had been working for some time, an epic piece entitled 'Totem Pole'. He wanted to have it recorded so he could play it on the gramophone he had, which had been bought for him by the Dublin novelist and screenwriter Maura Laverty. This gramophone was something of a miracle in Kimmage – no one else in the area owned one – and the Browns played 45s and 78s for many years on Laverty's gift. Christy was very concerned about the finished piece, and understandably so: Collis gave the poem to the writers Seán O'Faoláin and Cecil Day-Lewis and they both read it. Day-Lewis and Christy met again when he came to give a lecture at the Royal Dublin Society. He told Christy that the poem was 'essentially good, but that it contained far too much material'.

After reading and recording his work, as well as teaching him for many years in the 1950s, Dr Sheehan knew that Christy absorbed books like a sponge and was deeply influenced by whomever he was reading at the time. By the age of twenty-two, he had read the complete works of Dickens and of

Shakespeare and the Bible. She remembered how glad she was when he finished reading George Bernard Shaw and started on the poetry of Rupert Brooke. To Christy, though, who read Shaw straight after the works of Shakespeare: 'If meeting Shakespeare was like a breeze from heaven, meeting Shaw was like a fresh wind from the sea in March.'

When Sheehan visited Christy at Stannaway Road after he had left the clinic, her husband Bobby would drive her to the house and then he and 'Ma Brown' or 'Bid', as Bridget was often called, would chat in the kitchen while Dr Sheehan went out to Christy's study to talk to him. Sometimes, Christy would just want to gossip or have his poetry read aloud to him; at other times, he would simply want to be reassured that he had a friend in her. Then, after a while, 'the game would begin', as Sheehan described it: how long could he keep her away from Bobby? She felt that this was not done in 'any spiteful way', but rather as a boost to Christy's ego. Essentially, he wanted to see whether or not she was still interested in him. As she put it, the longer he could hold her attention, the more chuffed he was. Meanwhile Bobby and Ma would be getting on famously in the kitchen. Patricia felt that everyone, including Bobby, knew that Christy's game was 'harmless'. She believes that she never caused Christy a lustful thought. He knew that she was spoken for and she said he 'glowed in the reflection of the love Bobby and I showed each other and radiated to others'.

During 1956, Christy grew a beard, which he called his 'fungus', and his change of appearance was accompanied by a new artistic direction. He decided that the best way for him to become established as a serious author was to write a play. He gave a draft of a play (the title of which is no longer known) to the actress Ria Mooney, who was in the company of the Abbey Theatre. She read it and gave him 'every indication that the play would be accepted and put on sometime in 1958'. She told Christy that it needed some changes and alterations, and he agreed to take her suggestions seriously and to rework some parts of the dialogue. Ernest Blythe (the managing director of the Abbey Theatre in Dublin from 1941 to 1967) told Ria to tell Christy that he should be encouraged. Christy had decided that a career in the theatre was to be his new passion and, for him, this was a declaration of 'faith and acceptance'.

Ria came to Kimmage just before Christmas in 1956 to talk to him about the play and she again gave some indication that it would be put on in 1958. However, nothing ever came of it. He sent a different play to the BBC and was confident that he could get their attention, since he knew the Ulster poet W.R. Rodgers and his wife, who had produced a radio adaptation of *My Left Foot*. Nothing came of that either.

On 29 January 1957, Christy was contacted by Captain Seán Feehan of the Cork publishing house Mercier Press. Feehan ran the Irish branch of the Disabled Artists Association (DAA). In his experience as a publisher, he was familiar with Christy's writing and had heard of his painting; he was sure Christy should be persuaded to take his visual art more seriously.

The DAA was started by the German-born artist Arnulf Erich Stegmann in 1956. Stegmann was stricken with polio when he was three years old and lost the use of his hands and arms. He began to learn how to write, holding a pencil between his teeth. Using the same method, he learned how to paint and at a very early age was a star pupil in the art school he attended. When he was barely twenty years old, Stegmann's work was exhibited in several countries in Europe. As he became more successful, he took the initiative to make it his lifelong work to build up an alliance between disabled artists and to represent their interests worldwide. Christy was one of the first members of his organisation.

A week after he first contacted Christy, Feehan conducted an interview with him, looked at ten of his recent paintings and asked him to join the Disabled Artists Association, giving him two weeks to decide if he would like to work for them. He told Christy that he had to send his work to Herr Stegmann in Germany to see if he would hire him but suggested that this would not be a problem. After seeing his work, Stegmann was pleased to make Christy a member of the DAA. Feehan arranged for the organisation to pay for art lessons in Christy's home and a teacher, Mr Carroll, was sent out to give him instruction in painting.

The pay that the DAA offered Christy was good: £100 per month plus a percentage on the sale of each picture and its subsequent reproductions. He had to produce a certain number of paintings each year and keep up to the standard that Stegmann had set and approved. For Christy, £1,200 per year was a colossal income and this was in addition to his royalties from *My Left Foot*. An agent – Leonore, a twenty-six-year-old German woman – visited him in Kimmage once he had committed to the work, to give him his contract and explain all the necessary details. Leonore frequently came to the house and took Christy to the countryside to paint. He fell in love with her straight away, saying that he found it 'hard to concentrate when she's there beside me', because she was as 'exotic as her name'. He said that he 'at once began writing very melodramatic poems about her'. He felt lucky in that, as he wrote to Dr Sheehan:

> The whole thing seems above board, which makes the whole business more intriguing. It [the DAA] is probably run by a couple of eccentric millionaires with uncontrollable philanthropic leanings, who dodder about their gardens all day planting bulbs and cultivating geraniums with a view to extracting nuclear energy from them . . . very admirable lunatics, though.

But just the thought of dedicating most of his time to painting and giving up his writing in order to honour his commitments to the DAA upset Christy deeply; he was still working on plays, yet he was dissatisfied with most of them.

During the next five years, he would write to friends and other authors (such as the poets James Liddy and Raymond Roseliep) telling them how he loved the theatre more than anything or that what he wanted most was to be a poet. But it would always be his prose that brought him most success. He felt that 'even with proper training and education I would never be more than an average artist; on the other hand I had set my heart on becoming a rather good writer and poet . . . because writing is not only a passion – it is a necessity, as vital to my nature as the presence of beauty itself and the pursuit of beauty.' He felt writing was what he was really made for and that it was only writing that afforded him his truest means of self-expression and self-knowledge.

Christy's new novel, which would take him sixteen years to write, was already forming in his mind by 1958. His publishers often asked when his next book would be ready but his ideas were continually being reworked, both in his mind and on the page. In January 1959, he told Patricia Sheehan that he was writing a sequel to *My Left Foot* and that its subject matter wasn't 'so much a cripple endeavouring to overcome his handicaps, but rather an adult faced with the far more intimidating problem of overcoming himself after his handicap'. He planned to send some chapters to his British and American publishers to finance a visit to America to meet Beth Moore, a journey that he desperately wanted to make. Two years after joining the DAA, his funds from *My Left Foot* were running low and his DAA income was not going as far as he had anticipated. According to him, in a letter to Katriona, all his 'fabulous riches' had 'gone the way of the flesh'. Most of it had been spent in the pub.

On 4 May 1959, Barbara Bray, a script editor at the BBC (as well as a writer, translator and long-term lover of Samuel Beckett), wrote to thank Christy for sending her yet another play he had completed – an adaptation of a work called *The Hostelry*. Bray told him that she would be glad to consider it but the work was never produced.

By May 1959, Christy was exhausted. He had gone through a bad flu in March, developed sinusitis and then just as he recovered, he fell ill with the flu again. He had been working late into the night, which would become a lifelong habit, and he 'over drank'. Christy loved the night-time; he would sit for hours at night alone, reading and writing. Now, most often, he was with a bottle of alcohol. Often, after working hard through the night, Christy would take a break and drink more, looking at the letters Beth had sent to him and wondering about his future.

Chapter Seven

A LOVE AFFAIR

My Dearest,

It is an unconscious clod indeed who sleepwalks through life unassailed by doubts, untouched by fear, innocent of despair. Those of us who are by inclination or education articulate and analytical tend to ponder on the inequities and riddles of life, to verbalise our frustrations, hoping by this method to understand them and perhaps lessen them. There are also those whose circumstances of life haven't taught them to react this way but who feel the same doubts, fears and despair, not as clearly in their minds because they have never been carried beyond the state of emotional reactions. They might say they feel like hell and go out and get drunk. But because they don't have a clear picture of their conflicts, this doesn't mean they don't feel them of course, the more sensitive a person is, the more the subtle facets of life are recognised and appreciated by him. You are one of these sensitive people, and I don't think you'd want to be any different, and although you grieve more, you are also more in tune with beauty and joy . . .

. . . If I were to say, 'Of course it doesn't make any difference old man. You're imagining things,' you might accept it, but deep down you'd think that I was just trying to reassure you because I loved you. But the fact that I love you doesn't really enter into it. I should give the same answers to the same questions asked by anyone, because I truly believe these things to be so . . . And I should like

to remind you of that other fact, which I have no doubt of,
and which is the pole star of my existence, that I love you.
If it were possible for me to say how much, I fear there'd be
a large hole in the paper about here, with charred edges.
Onion skin can't stand heat you know.
    Your,
    Beth

Beth Moore, writing to Christy Brown,
27 October 1959

The letters exchanged between Beth and Christy show
a deep connection based on their romantic natures and
love of literature. Short, friendly letters had begun their
correspondence. Beth spoke of her admiration for Christy and
he told her of his desire to be as educated as her. But in only a
few years, they began exchanging confessional pages of their
loneliness and fears. Like Christy, Beth was trapped, in her case
in a loveless marriage, which she refused to leave because of
her three young children. They would write to each other on
a weekly basis for years and often one of them would become
panicked if they had not heard from the other in the space of
a week. She would write to him of how she spent her days
– editing high-school textbooks, taking literature classes at
local colleges and writing poetry, which was never published.
She read his work and offered him honest but loving advice.
She also gave him personal, sometimes stern guidance. She
often told him to eat well, ease up on the drinking and not be
so emotionally erratic. Beth would often ask his advice too;
she considered becoming a physical therapist and wondered
if he thought it was a good idea. His letters to her are lost.
One imagines their connection to have been more powerful
in that it existed at first on paper – they were one another's
anonymous confidants. And their physical distance from one
another, as well as the enormous distances between them in
terms of class, culture and religion, allowed them more space
for romanticising one another in their minds. Eventually, they

would sleep with one another, spend time in one another's homes and meet one another's families, pretending to be just friends. Their relationship was always guarded and secretive; although Beth was terrified of losing her family, she risked it. In 1959, Christy confided to Patricia Sheehan that he was engaged and that he 'hadn't actually met her yet', but that, he wrote, was his 'number one reason for going to America'.

That May, he stopped painting and writing. He went to stay in a hospital in Finglas, County Dublin, for six weeks to recover from the exhaustion he was suffering as a result of flu, drinking and late nights. When he got back, there was good news waiting for him. The DAA teacher who worked with Christy, Mr Carroll, resumed his lessons and told him that one of his pictures had been accepted by the organisation to be reproduced in card form, which was quite rare. Indeed, having a card printed was normally conditional on the artist being a fully fledged member of the DAA, which, despite the commitment he had shown, Christy was not.

Christy's tendency to drink for hours whilst contemplating the great questions of life and its purpose (particularly in relation to his illness) were in full force in 1959. He had decided to keep his beard and by October he had written a short story for the Marrowbone Lane Fund. He was by now seen in the wider world as living proof that disabled people could lead their own fruitful lives.

In the last week of May 1960, just before Christy was supposed to leave for America to stay with Beth Moore and her family for six weeks, Bridget suffered a burst ulcer and had a heart attack. She was taken to St Kevin's Hospital in Dublin. Bridget was fifty-nine years old and the doctors decided to keep her in the hospital for X-rays to determine whether or not an operation would be necessary. Christy was supposed to go to America on 26 July but he decided to await the results of his mother's tests before deciding whether or not to travel. He went to stay with his eldest brother, Tony, in Ballyfermot and after his mother was given the all clear, there was a rush to get his passport, photos and money sorted out.

One of the local priests ended up driving Christy to the American Embassy to help him get his visa and make the appropriate arrangements for his travels. The priest presumed, as Christy was in his wheelchair and the office which they had to go to was up several flights of stairs, that it would be best if he took the paperwork up himself and explained the situation. The office worker refused to hand over the visa unless it was signed by Christy himself, so the priest went back to Christy and told him the problem. Christy told him to carry him up to the secretary and when he arrived, he did not let the priest speak for him. Instead, he asked him only to help him remove his left shoe. When he did so, Christy asked the secretary to place a pen between his toes and as she watched aghast, he signed all the necessary documents. Christy and the priest laughed together for hours afterwards, thinking of the shock on the woman's face.

Christy was thrilled at the idea of going to America. He had always wanted to travel and Beth had written many letters to him talking about what they would do if he came to visit her. Christy's trip was funded by the Houseman & Son Foundation in New York, which provided grants for people with cerebral palsy to go to the United States, either to develop their careers or to receive treatment. Beth had contacted them on behalf of Christy and then he had written to them telling them he intended to write a book based on his experiences in America. They paid for his fare and living expenses.

The United Cerebral Palsy Association, meanwhile, had planned a whole day of events in honour of him, which they were calling Christy Brown Day. He thought this was hilarious. It was, he said to Beth in one of his letters, 'damn nice of them' but he was scared stiff at the prospect of having to give speeches or represent himself in any way. He told Katriona that he was no campaigner or advocate for sufferers of cerebral palsy; he was 'just an ordinary cripple with an ordinary story and very ordinary brains, with a rather more than ordinary like for alcohol'.

Christy met Robert Collis at the airport on 26 July as planned and the doctor flew with him from Dublin. Christy thought the fifteen-hour overnight journey very tiring but the 'delightful hostess' on the plane helped speed things along nicely for him. Beth (or Betty, as he most often called her) got up at five in the morning and drove (on her own) to meet Christy and Collis at Idlewild Airport in New York. This was their first meeting in person. She wore an orange print dress and as he and Collis came out of the arrivals hall, she threw her hands in the air as a victory salute.

The Moore home on Long Island was an imposing, fifty-year-old colonial house. It was surrounded by five acres of land, which were covered in elms, oaks, beech and pine trees. The house had fourteen bedrooms and a private beach almost on its doorstep. The Moores also owned two boats. Christy was shocked at the size of everything in America and thrown by US fashions and the way of life there. He loved watching girls walking around in their short shorts (something one would never see in Dublin). One afternoon, two 'luscious and curvaceous' girls passed him in small outfits, smiling, and shouted to him, 'Hi there!' He tried to imagine the same thing happening in Kimmage, he wrote to Katriona, and 'failed utterly'.

During the first few days he got to know Beth's family, including her husband, Deac, and became used to his new surroundings. However, watching Beth in her home disturbed him. For five years, they had shared 'an intense and candid' correspondence and now here he was seeing her in person. He believed that they knew one another better than most couples, because their secretive letters were so deeply personal. He also believed that their bond was all the more intimate for its lack of physical exchange and experience. He was frightened because he had travelled three thousand miles to 'test a dream, an ideal, and face a challenge'. He thought that perhaps he would be let down but he was also happier than he had ever been. The illusory and dream-like nature of their relationship (and he admits to his friends in his letters that to a certain degree it was an illusion) was shattered and he and Beth were all the better for it. Sharing the experience of getting to know one another in person, facing his physical challenges as a couple and simply being with one another made them fall even more deeply in love.

Physically, Christy had never had to be self-reliant to the extent required by the trip. Yet he fell into the American lifestyle with tremendous ease and enthusiasm. He dressed and undressed himself. (This was easier than it might have been, for, as he wrote to Katriona, 'Americans wear so little in the summer'.) He swam every day with the help of a cylindrical inflated tube. Beth would usually swim alongside him, pushing him along. He bathed himself without any help.

Some discoveries were simply revelations. The use of a straw, for instance, changed his daily life. Christy loved to drink but before he began using straws, he had to have someone pick up his glass or cup and put it to his lips or, when he was alone at night, struggle to manage a bottle with his left foot. Now, all he had to do was ask for a refill. He drank iced tea, Tom Collinses, cold beer and ('inevitably', he said) Irish whiskey. For the rest of his life, after that trip to America, Christy would use a straw to drink with. His brother Paddy remembers how, after he returned from Connecticut, 'every one of the brothers had a straw somewhere in his pocket' in case Christy needed one or forgot one of his own (which, Paddy said, 'he never did'). His brother Seán says they would sometimes stick a pea in the bottom of his straw, just to see how long it would take for Christy to figure it out, and they would have a great laugh about it.

In America, Christy also discovered Velcro, which made an

enormous difference to his dressing and undressing himself. As he wrote to Katriona:

> But it is the way in which I have come to be able to help myself that will delight you the most. In fact the whole experience has been an object-lesson in physical self-education and self-help. Thanks to the ingenuity of Beth and Deac I can now do things I never did before – dressing myself almost completely, taking a bath whenever I like, feeding myself in the day time when I am alone, brushing my teeth thoroughly each morning . . . You just wouldn't believe it! The dressing is made possible by means of a material called Vel-cro, which Beth has sewn onto my shirts and pants, in parallel strips on each side which cling when pressed together – I'll show you how it is done when I get home. In fact, I am just about self-contained now and can function almost independently. This I need not tell you is a tremendous boost to my morale and has put me in great spirits. I know my mother will be delighted out of her wits at all I can do for myself now. I am dying to get home to show them all and to brag boastfully and unmercifully!

Christy's desire to travel and see new things had been with him since he was young, evident in the letters he had written to Katriona as a teenager. Now that he had the chance, he took every opportunity that Beth presented to him to go out and do new things. The United Cerebral Palsy Association held a luncheon for him on a ranch in the Catskill Mountains and he went to a symposium at the Waldorf-Astoria in New York, sponsored by some world body (the name of which he did not care to remember because they styled themselves an 'organisation for the welfare of cripples'). At the latter event, he drank cocktails in a downstairs lounge until three in the morning. He laughed as a 'treacly tenor' sang with a 'pseudo-Irish cadence' 'Believe Me, If All Those Endearing Young Charms' and was even more amused watching the 'barn dance performed by crippled couples in wheelchairs'.

Most of his trips to New York City took place at night but on one day trip he and Beth drove through the Bronx, Brooklyn, Queens, Times Square, Broadway, downtown Manhattan and Wall Street (which he thought very dull and depressing). On the same day, he visited the United Nations, a tour he particularly enjoyed because of a 'luscious girl guide from Tennessee with a southern drawl and limpid blue eyes'. While there, he lunched in the delegates' dining hall, where he and Beth met Dr Collis. Afterwards, Beth and Christy went to the top of the Empire State Building and took a ferry trip around Manhattan Island.

Together, he and Beth saw *The Music Man* and several other Broadway shows. They also watched Katharine Hepburn and Robert Ryan in *Antony and Cleopatra* at the Stratford Festival in New Haven. Christy thought that Hepburn was phenomenal, as he wrote to Katriona: ' . . . she's 56 if she's a day and yet there she was prancing around the stage with girlish agility and making love with flamboyant recklessness and ardour'. In all, he went to New York six times during his six-week stay in the USA.

Christy adored all the small New England villages he went to, such as New Bedford, which reminded him of scenes from the writings of Hawthorne and Twain. On the days when he was not sightseeing, he would go to beach parties, drink bourbon, sing songs and eat huge steaks, hot dogs and pizzas. When whoever he was with would ask for a song, he would give them 'The Sally Gardens' (a traditional Irish tune with lyrics by Yeats) or 'Kevin Barry' (a song about a young man who was killed by British soldiers in 1920 and who had actually been a neighbour of Christy's mother on Old North King Street).

As Christy described the holiday to Patricia Sheehan:

> those evenings were unforgettable, in a sort of blue and
> silver world where hardly a breeze stirred, and I can still

see the moonlight glimmering on the waveless waters of the sound and the stars hanging like opals overhead, and the frank friendly faces of the people around me lit by the flames from the spiralling bonfires – one among them that meant something deep and beautiful to me.

When he came back to Kimmage, Christy drank a great deal. He was irritable and obstreperous when dealing with his mother. He told Katriona that he felt trapped in a 'snail-like, cul-de-sac' world. He craved freedom and he wanted to be with Beth. Her absence was driving him crazy. Christy was a true romantic. He always wanted to be in love and now that he had found someone to love, she was thousands of miles away and married. He told Sheehan that the problem was not that of meeting the right one; the trouble was that, 'as ever, someone met her before' him. His reaction was simply 'and so it goes', yet underneath he was devastated. Beth and he were truly in love; he told Katriona in a letter written on 6 October 1960, two weeks after coming home:

> It seems one of the inexorable rules of life is that we do not fully appreciate our happiness and joys until they are taken away from us; it was certainly so with me. I had to leave Beth before I realised with such inner pain and truth just how much she meant to me. She above all others had loved me and the individual man in me, and my disability was merely a secondary factor and a subject of wry humour and candid managing. Never before had I been aware of such wholeness and completeness in myself. With her, nothing was impossible, no task too great, no ideal too remote . . . one woman had shown me it is possible – possible to build a life outside my family, to love and be loved, not through the focus lens of imaginary experience, but in the forge of life and reality, through the direct and living agency of body and soul.

He was heartbroken at having to leave Beth. At home, for weeks, he was bad-tempered and ill-mannered (he told Katriona in letters that he felt particularly guilty about behaving badly towards his mother). Eventually, he started to focus on his work in order to pull himself out of his depression.

Chapter Eight

A WRITER

And so it goes. This is my life, from typewriter to easel and back again, day by day, week by week, with occasional sallies down to my local pub in search of oblivion, which, however, only leads at times to even deeper creative urges! A lot of good people are irreconcilably convinced that poor old C. Brown has become so addicted to the bottle that he'll never write anything of value again. Personally, I never felt better, and fully intend to go on drinking and writing for as long as I am able.

You may get some idea of what I mean when I tell you that when Dr Collis saw my New York publishers in June one of the chief editors said to him, 'Pity abut poor old Christy – whatever happened to him? Drinking himself into the grave – regular Van Gogh he became.' It took Bob some time to assure him that he had left me a week previously, working happily away and in the best of health . . . that sort of number has got around Dublin more than once, but I was really quite flattered to know that my alleged debaucheries had been reported as far as New York! Ah, fame what indeed is thy spur.

Christy Brown, writing to Katriona Maguire,
1961

In the first half of the 1960s, Christy was drinking heavily, working hard and enjoying his life. His younger brother Francis remembers taking him into the city for a pub crawl and Christy becoming obnoxious, as he usually did. So he left Christy in his wheelchair on the street. 'Fuck ya,' he told him, 'you're an eejit. You can find your own way home.' Many of the family's acquaintances have told similar anecdotes. The Browns' friend Maura Mahon (whose sister was married to the eldest son of the family, Tony) remembers evenings with Christy and his mother as some of the best nights out she ever had. On one occasion, Maura had driven to the pub, where Bridget, Christy and she drank quite a bit. They all sang together on the way home and when they arrived, something set Bridget and Maura off laughing. Having drunk so much and being nearly helpless with laughter, they had a hard time helping Christy out of Maura's car. Bridget said to him, 'Come on, son, try and get your feet off the ground, come on.' Christy couldn't stand up at all. Maura told him, 'We're all jarred, Christy, you know. You're not the only one, we all need a bit of help.'

The three of them only had to get up three steps into the house at Stannaway Road. But again, someone made a joke and they all started laughing. They laughed so hard they fell over into the garden. The three of them lay there roaring with laughter but it was Christy, 'the invalid', as Maura puts it, who had to yell at them, 'Will ye pull yourselves together!'

Maura remembers that when he shouted at them, it was as if he hadn't had a drink and he must have had a terrible fright, thinking that they would all end up sleeping in the garden. He carried on, telling them, 'You never know who could pass by, Ma! Jesus, Mary and Joseph, what's wrong with youse two tonight.' Bridget replied, 'I don't care who passes. You can fall into your own garden, can't ya?'

Some of the letters Christy received during the 1960s were indicative of the wild nights he was having. Paul Muldoney of the *Evening Press* wrote to him with the following message:

Dear Mr Brown,

A woman rang to say that what she believes is the missing part of your invalid chair is 'stuck in the hedge' of her front garden. She refused to give her name or address, but asked that you ring her (3———) after 6 p.m.

We hope that you are successful. You might favour us with a phone call if it is the missing part. Our number is 7——— and ask for the News Editor of the *Evening Press*.

Although Christy was out drinking a lot and it appeared to the world that he was happy, internally he was devoured by demons. What he wanted more than anything was to produce a piece of art that would last in time, one that would give him great stature in the literary world and make people think about him in terms other than the boy who had been 'rescued' by Robert Collis and had 'overcome the odds'. At the beginning of May 1961, Christy and Dr Sheehan went to a fund-raiser for the Cerebral Palsy Clinic held in the ballroom of the Shelbourne Hotel, where the famous Irish writers Brendan Behan and John B. Keane held a debate on the nature of Irish theatre. Struck by the evening, he wrote to Patricia a few days later:

I'm sorry I failed to write after that evening among the theatrical goliaths of the contemporary – or should I say semi-contemporary? – Irish Drama . . . Now from this point in time it all seems rather hazy and remote – seen that is through a Celtic Twilight of alcohol.

Behan must have been his usual ebullient self, surely? He never says anything very profound, for that would be completely out of character, and no matter what we say about him he always is in character, isn't he? What he does say, however, he says very well and with a verve and vivacity that could not be equalled save by an early O'Casey and even then with much less colour.

I think Behan has more colour than ever O'Casey [did], except that he's a clumsy artist and splashes his paints all over the canvas, making a lot go a very little way. Beside him, John B. Keane seemed rather puerile and bodyless, like Hamlet and the Ghost, though no doubt he is a very fine playwright even if he does choose such macabre and depressing subjects for his drama. He is a poet in the Synge tradition, a traditionalist where Behan is an ardent contemporary, for all his resemblance to O'Casey, whose Dublin, after all, is as dead as Joyce's – that is if Joyce ever had a Dublin. That, though, isn't the important thing about O'Casey, nor is it the important thing about Behan; I'm quite sure both of them will be read, seen and duly criticised forty, fifty or even a hundred years from now, because it wasn't what they observed and wrote about in their own history which will matter, but how they observed and how they wrote. I suppose that is true of all genuine artists . . . their ability to make the living word, the living brush stroke, stay alive long after the minds which produced them are gone.

Ray McAnally [the actor], as I expected, came down very decidedly on the part of Keane, since his (Keane's) – brand of drama has always been the real lifeblood of The Abbey, ever since 'The Playboy' nearly caused its destruction at the turn of the century. 'With your long arm and your strong arm would you be after pulling me a pint of solid stout, Padeen Joe . . .' And so on. Whereas Mr Behan, cutting out the patent poetry, would simply say: 'Jasus, I'm gasping' . . . it seems to me that our Behan is much less in danger of getting left behind than that bold mountainy gentleman Mr Keane.

Christy dwells here on the status of individual writers in the Irish canon and on the treatment they can expect to receive from posterity and this is indicative of his anxiety about his own position. Although he was a successful writer, a well-known figure in Dublin literary society and a friend of Behan's, he was tormented by the fear that he had not yet written something that would 'be read, seen and duly criticised forty, fifty or even a hundred years from now'. The debate had also reminded him of his continuing outsider status. He had watched but could say nothing and he was angry because he was unable to express himself in the moment.

Throughout the early 1960s, he became determined to put new work into print. He wanted to be recognised as an intellectual. With Dr Collis, he had been working on a play entitled *Mrs Brennan* throughout 1959 and 1960. By the end of 1961, he scrapped it and started working on his own on a new play, entitled *The Hotel*. He gave up on *Mrs Brennan* largely because of its language. Christy and Collis had used a 'Dublinese' dialogue and when Christy reread the text, he was annoyed by the stylised quality of the language, which seemed to him dry and disingenuous. Collis had a strong influence on his work and inspired him but Christy had different ideas about Dublin and art. He told Katriona Maguire in a letter:

> I admire Collis. Please get that right. I am perhaps more indebted to him than my pride would like; but I acknowledge that debt, whole-heartedly and with thanks. Yet, I do believe that our so-called literary collaboration was never more than a myth anyway. The simple facts being that he very happily happened to be the hand that released the floodgates of my mental energies, for which I will be forever grateful, but to which I do not consider myself forever tied. His idea of a play, written by the two of us, is wildly different from mine, and I think that the gulf is pretty unbridgeable.
>
> His sense of humour, his conception of what is funny and what is not, always in a Dublin sense, as I believe this is going to be a Dublin play . . . well as I say we look at it from different sides of the fence: I mean for God's sake, what more disastrous combination could you have than someone in the 'upper-class' bending over backwards to appreciate the humour at the other end of the scale, and a member of the working-class gallantly struggling to produce dialogue that would appeal to the

'upper classes'. Never the twain shall meet, as far as I am concerned . . . I have come a million years since the mid-nineteen-fifties when modestly I appeared upon the literary scene and I think I owe it to myself to prove it. Which you might recollect I am in the process of doing.

In January 1962, Christy's typewriter was failing. Iron Sally was 'dying', so he wrote to IBM (who had taken over J.A. Miller & Son) asking for a new one. As he was losing his familiar working tool, new ideas flowed in. In February, he sent a play to the BBC and wrote to the literary magazine *Argos* in London. He placed great hopes for publication in what he perceived as the avant-garde character of the journal and he sent them some short stories. Their writers included Frank O'Connor, Graham Greene and Seán O'Faoláin, so Christy felt that he would be in great company. *Argos* rejected his stories but he continued to write to Irish theatres, newspapers and journals looking for work. In March, IBM sent on a good second-hand typewriter, which was in excellent condition and had just had a new motor fitted. Christy called it 'Battling Betsy' after Beth Moore; the name also reflected his frustration in trying to get his work out into the world. There was still a trickle of money coming in from *My Left Foot* and from his work with the DAA but instead of being careful with his money, he bought himself a car (a 1955 Wolseley 444, the cost of which he shared with his brother Eamonn) and hired a friend to drive him around.

In the first week of October 1962, Christy wrote to Liam Miller of the Dolmen Press in Dublin asking him if he might consider printing any of his poems. Miller wrote back saying that he could not afford to produce another book of verse any time soon but he advised Christy to write to James Liddy, the editor of a magazine called *Poetry Ireland*. On 7 October, Christy wrote back to Miller thanking him for his suggestion and including 'random instances' for Miller to look at, in the hope that they might nonetheless be published. Christy had never heard of *Poetry Ireland* but he wrote to them to enquire if they would be interested in publishing his work.

Although he was struggling to get new work accepted, the media had not lost interest in the man behind *My Left Foot*. On 18 October, the RTÉ television show *Radharc* (meaning 'perspective' or 'viewpoint' in English) aired a programme with Christy as its main feature. The documentary was based on interviews with Christy and his mother. The journalists asked Bridget how she coped with working and having so many children. They asked Christy how he managed to keep a positive attitude about his life and what he felt about his paintings and writings. After watching the show, he was reasonably happy. He told Katriona that he hated the way his face contorted on camera and that he hoped his voice had been clear enough to be understood. When his speech was being recorded, the presence of the microphone and the knowledge that it would be aired had made him tense. But he loved seeing his paintings on screen and was pleased that they looked 'quite professional'. What touched him most when watching the show was seeing that Katriona had kept the first letter that he had written to her 'in my left-foot scrawl'. It brought back old memories and made him wonder at his own achievements.

At the end of 1962, Christy was in full swing writing *The Hotel*. He was working alone this time and found it deeply satisfying. He was glad to be rid of Collis's ideas about what made something funny and he knew his ear for language had developed far beyond most people's. His condition had forced him all his life to sit, listen and observe and because he had watched and learned about Dublin and its culture for so long, his characters were real and their speech genuine. Christy wrote to Katriona about the work's progress:

> I've been meaning to write you for ages but never seem to get down to this very pleasant task . . . every day is taken up with work. My play is finished as such, and only needs some rewriting in patches. It's the rewriting

that takes the wind out you, for on reading the supposed finished article ever you feel you always want to scrap every page of it and rewrite it as a whole with the conviction – not always accurate – that you can do a better job second time around, so to speak. Anyway, it is finished by and large and when I've rounded it off to my satisfaction I'm sending it to Ray McAnally of the Abbey . . .

I have written a play which is the exact opposite of the Collis method – no unoffending dialogue, no daring use of the expletive 'bloody', no morning coffee. I have set this play in a decaying old Georgian tenement house on the Quays that once gloried in being one of the smartest guesthouses in Dublin. People still refer to it as The Hotel – and that's my title for it. The time is the present, but it could be anytime, for the lives of these city-dwellers don't change much even over a period of years, and they still lead the same sort of lives as they lived before, during and after 1922. World wars matter very little to them except in the loss of a husband or son, and no matter what government holds office they must still eke out a living on the docks or on building sites or carting scrap iron and metal around the city in handcarts. Theirs is a timeless sort of existence, and in this belief my play doesn't end with any neatly arrived at conclusion or denouement – it simply goes on as in the beginning, like life itself, no matter what dark tragic things have happened in the meantime. I explore with varying depth nearly the gamut of human emotion from the tender bloom and pain of first love to brutal lust and violence, all imbued with the taste and the taint of poverty and its appalling effects on the human personality.

I don't exalt poverty, for we're not all Francis of Assisi and far from breeding any talent or genius in a person I believe poverty merely breeds tuberculosis and stultifies whatever natural talents you possess. (Personally I always write or paint better with a full belly or when I can look forward to a few pints afterwards.) The dialogue in this play may seem shocking to some unbroken minds, but believe me, I haven't invented it just for effect. I hear it frequently, day after day in fact, and it never fails to enthral me. It isn't mere vulgarity, it certainly isn't conscious vulgarity – it's simply a mode of self-expression that is as natural and unforced as any other. These people – the sort of people in my play – don't express ideas in talk, but emotions, feelings, what they're actually feeling and going through at the exact moment of expression. Life is too immediate for any leisurely reflection – they're too caught up with life to think about it much, so on the surface it would appear that they lead shallow and superficial lives with no time for thought of philosophy, and therefore if and when this play is put on it may seem shallow and superficial as well, but that's only because whenever you deal with what people are doing instead of with what people are thinking you always run the risk of being called superficial. I'd like you to read this play, but I've just one copy and I don't want to lose time in letting McAnally see it! You may not want to call me your friend afterwards, for I am no longer the author of *My Left Foot* and my public image may be somewhat tarnished by this bizarre piece of drama, that is if I ever possessed such an exotic commodity as a public image. Still, to thine own self be true, and I'm being just that in the writing of *The Hotel*. Wish me luck!

In the first week of November 1960, James Liddy told Christy that the editorial board of *Poetry Ireland* (consisting of himself and the poets James J. McAuley and Richard Weber) had looked at his work and thought that the most achieved poem he had sent was 'Sunlight and Shadow'. They also liked 'Autumnal' and 'In Retrospect' and were considering publishing them, if Christy would remove some of the overly romantic and verbose characteristics of his style. They wanted the language to be 'harder and more specific'. Liddy reminded him that 'a poem must not lose a word to imprecision'. Christy was pleased about finally being able to make headway as a poet and on 10 November 1962, he replied to Liddy's expression of interest, writing that he would certainly take on board his advice (Liddy had specifically suggested that Christy alter lines which he deemed 'soft'). At the end of the year, *Poetry Ireland* agreed to put out his poem 'Frostbite' (the first line of which is 'I might have made a poem out of this') in the spring edition of the magazine and *Arena* agreed to publish another of his poems, 'The Lost Prize'.

Meanwhile, in late November, Katriona gave Christy a copy of *Brendan Behan's Island*, a collection of the writer's reminiscences and anecdotes, and he was very excited to read it. He wrote to her saying that Brendan was

> really a phenomenon and we should all be proud that he is one of us. Can Britain or America offer anything in the same category? By hell they can't. He's the greatest literary artist in Europe today and you have to go all the way back to Trollope to find a writer who can create such rollicking and bombastic characters. He has a Shakespearean zeal and gust for the ribald, the boisterous, the delightfully amoral, the magnificent riff-raff and outcasts of society. It will take several generations to replace him, I'm telling you, for the likes of Behan are as rare as Halley's comet, and compared to mediocre mortals and writers like myself he rises like a Colossus dwarfing us with his mere shadow. He has a bit to go before he has the verve, the vivacity and the sheer strength of O'Casey in 'Juno', but that he will reach those heights and soon I have no doubts at all, and what's more I think he'll have a longer and livelier existence than O'Casey ever had. I can't see Behan degenerating into a bitter and spiteful old man in an Aran woollen jacket and cap spitting venom at his native country and endeavouring to justify himself with pathetic echoes of a once mighty talent. No. Behan will produce masterpiece after masterpiece before he drops dead suddenly, full of gargle and laughter. He'll go out

like a light, not like a flickering candle, and not before he has lit a light that will take many a long day to go out . . . Forgive the eulogy! It's just that we poor native writers and poets and artists are so unaccustomed to native praise or recompense that I feel we ought to belong to some union to protect ourselves.

Christy's relationship with Behan was a strange one. Behan's family, like the Browns, had been moved to Kimmage from the city-centre tenements. In his short radio play *Moving Out*, Behan has a character ask a bus driver where Kimmage is on the line; 'Siberia' is the response. The two writers had much in common and they began to drink together after the publication of *My Left Foot* (later, they'd both be allowed to drink for free in the Stone Boat in Kimmage, in the hope that the presence of two famous local characters would encourage more customers to come in). Christy's family remember Behan often calling at their house on Stannaway Road, carrying with him a box of bottles of Guinness and shouting at Christy that he was only successful because he was in a wheelchair and that he wished he had been a cripple himself. Christy's sister Ann says: 'Brendan used to come up to me mammy's house from the pub across the road – it used to be called Floyd's and Brendan used to drink there. He used to come up to our house at four o' clock in the day after having a few jars; he used to call in for Christy with half a dozen beers, you know, the way they used to sell beer in the old bottles with the corks. I was very young at the time, this was in the early '60s, and he'd come in, a big stack of a man and he'd be jarred. Mother would try to sober him up and he'd be pulling out these bottles of Guinness and giving them to Christy.'

Bridget would sometimes kick Behan out of the house but all in all the family liked him because they found him funny and tough. As Paddy Brown remembers, he was like everyone else in Kimmage, he was 'rough and ready', because 'you had to be back then'. As Behan became more successful (with his play *The Hostage* (1958) being produced in London and his autobiography *Borstal Boy* (1958) becoming an internationally well-received book in the early '60s), Christy would sing his praises in some letters and in others condemn him as an entertaining buffoon. Robert Collis had had an influence on Behan, too. When he was in borstal, he had read *The Silver Fleece* and been mesmerised by it. So the two had many things in common and until Christy wrote a work that could compete with his, Behan would remain a constant reminder that he could do more and had not.

In March 1963, Christy finished his play *The Hotel*. It was a tragedy in three acts, set in an old tenement house nicknamed 'the Hotel' by its tenants. The plot revolved around one family in particular and the effect the father had on it. He was excited about the possibility of *The Hotel* being staged and he sent it to Ray McAnally, one of the established actors in the company of the Abbey Theatre, who had agreed to read it as a friend and give Christy his honest opinion on it. Christy had hopes of being the first playwright to have a work produced in the Abbey Theatre's new building, to be opened in 1966. Ray McAnally had high praise for *The Hotel* but he told Christy that there were too many plays mixed up in it. He advised him to try and find one single compelling theme in it and then he thought it might work. Christy accepted his advice but gave up on the play being produced at the Abbey, deciding that it was 'not an Abbey play by any stretch of the imagination'. McAnally said he would send it on to Alan Simpson, who ran smaller theatres in Dublin, for his consideration. Christy was more than satisfied with this, as Alan Simpson had been the first to put on Behan's play *The Quare Fellow*, at the Pike Theatre, and Christy admired the production and hoped to achieve something as challenging and brave in its content as Behan's play. In the end, the play was never produced but much of the material in it would eventually find its way into *Down All the Days*. Coincidentally, twenty-five years later, McAnally would play the role of Christy's father in the film version of *My Left Foot* and the performance would earn him worldwide recognition and the attention of Hollywood producers.

In a letter to Katriona, Christy writes about having seen an adaptation of John McGahern's *The Barracks* in 1963 in Dublin. He was impressed by the play but adopted a rather affected tone in his comments, arguing that 'sometimes to be miscast is the greatest test of the actor's skill'. Christy was adamant that one day he would have one of his plays produced and the same letter makes his ambitions clear:

> I really must . . . write a play before I become too senile to write a postscript. I have always been fascinated by the theatre, it is such an enormously audacious thing to try and captivate an entire audience of several hundred people all at once and purely by your own creative endeavours.

But he certainly knew all the tricks that captivate audiences. Albeit involuntarily, he had been on stage since his birth and he makes a passing remark in the last section of the letter about the cathartic effect of performing: 'It must be very exhilarating to one's insatiable ego.'

By October 1963, Christy was painting three pictures a week. He was trying to write whilst enduring 'the travelling showman act' of painting in public for the DAA, which made him 'feel like a performing barrel-organ monkey'. The motives of the organisation for asking him to paint in public were primarily to do with publicity. These mobile exhibitions, in which he was asked to paint in front of an audience, drove him mad. The touring schedule was also quite rigorous. He was taken to town halls, convents and hospitals, doing two or three shows a week. Still, he was grateful for the £40 a month it provided him with.

The DAA's representative in Ireland, Seán Feehan, had agreed with Christy, in his role as managing director of

Mercier Press, that they would release *My Left Foot* in a paperback edition and Christy added a new chapter to it, replacing Robert Collis's original foreword. He earned 10 per cent on each copy sold, which he worked out as six old pence on each five-shilling copy. As Mercier planned on issuing 10,000 copies, Christy was excited about the potential jump in his income.

Feehan also took the writer Ulick O'Connor to meet Christy at the family home in Kimmage. O'Connor came in with Feehan, said hello and introduced himself to Ann. He then asked if he could meet Christy. Ann knew Christy wasn't up to it, as he had been out drinking the night before. So she told him, 'Ah, well, he's staying at my brother's house, he stayed over after having a few jars.' It was all she could think of off the top of her head. She told them he might be back that evening. So they sat talking for about half an hour and then Feehan asked Ann if they could just take a look at Christy's study before they went. 'Aw, Jesus,' she thought, 'he's in bed.' Ann started to go red. She was very embarrassed and she told Feehan and O'Connor to hang on for a minute. She went out to the study and told Christy, 'Jesus Christ, Ulick O'Connor is here and I'm after telling him you're at your brother's!' He started to laugh at her and said, 'Ah, you were caught out!' All of a sudden, Ulick and Feehan were stood behind her and she just said, 'Well, what can I say?' The friendship between Christy and Ulick that began that day would last until the day Christy died.

Ann also remembers that Freddie May, a minor celebrity who was often on the Irish radio shows, used to call to Stannaway Road so often that the family got 'sick of him'. He used to come out every week, to play the piano. He was a tiny man and always wore shoes that didn't match. The Browns would hide from him and run out to Christy's study, telling him 'Oh, here's this mad fucker! Your mad musician friend is here!' Christy would reply, 'Tell him I'm not fucking here.' May would then kneel down and shout through the letterbox, 'I know youse are there! Open the door!'

According to Ann, there was also a young man called Martin who used to try to be 'matey' with Christy. Martin had cerebral palsy but, as Ann puts it, 'Christy didn't hang around with disabled people, he only went to the clinic, and they didn't make firm friends because it wasn't in his head to be disabled. He felt he was normal, that he wasn't a disabled person.' Martin's cerebral palsy was much better than Christy's. He could walk but his knees would drop underneath him and then he'd bob up and then he'd drop on his knees again. The Browns used to say, 'Here's your mate that goes on his knees!' He used to come out to the house, and Bridget would tell the children, 'Ah, here, bring them down to the Stone Boat. I'm not able for this fella here all night.' So Christy, Martin and Willy (Ann's husband) would go to the pub and Willy would take Christy to the toilet while Martin would walk to the bar to get a few drinks but, as the joke went, by the time he got there, he was on his knees.

Part of the reason Christy loved drinking was that his speech would become more relaxed and, as Ann puts it, he didn't 'have to hold himself'. He liked watching other people slur their words and lose control of their bodies; it made him feel comfortable. His brothers and sisters understood his speech more easily after he had had a few drinks, because of the muscle relaxation induced by the alcohol, and after a few jars he could sing quite well. His mother would always try to curtail his drinking. Most often, Christy started with pints of Guinness and then moved on to shots. When they were in the pub together, Christy's mother would drown his vodka in lemonade.

In some respects his fame served to exacerbate his drinking. Other drinkers would buy him pints and in his locals he was often given free drink. Once, his sister Mona and her husband Tom went with Christy to a pub in Drumcondra, an area of Dublin where he would not have been known. After finding some seats, Tom went up to the bar to get two pints and the bartender looked at Tom and said, 'I'll give you a pint but that fella with you has had enough.' Tom just went back to his seat, while Christy started demanding his drink. Tom told him that the bartender said he wouldn't serve him. Christy shouted, 'Where is my fucking pint?' Christy complained so loudly that someone in the pub explained to the man who Christy was and about his writing and painting. He came down to them, all apologies, and he didn't take anything for the pints.

In 1964, two more of Christy's poems, 'Echo' and 'Surf', were published by *Arena* in their summer issue. A small publication called *The Holy Door* followed on from *Arena*, taking up its idea of presenting new Irish writing and writers. The writer Brian Lynch was running the poetry magazine, the ethos of which was a rejection of stereotypically Irish, clichéd writing. The artists who ran the magazine (Lynch, James Liddy and Michael Hartnett) wanted to publish work that reflected Ireland's relationship to Europe. *The Holy Door* was 'devoted to the new mind and the new eye', and presented a new and more sophisticated idea of Irish writing to the public. Only three editions were put out but many prominent poets and writers were published in those three issues, including W.H. Auden, Paul Durcan, Patrick Kavanagh, John Montague, Pablo Neruda (translated by Robert Bly) and Andrei Voznesensky (also in translation).

Lynch went to Kimmage to meet Christy in 1965 and they ended up drinking in the Stone Boat, where Lynch watched Christy drink Guinness after Guinness. After a few rounds, they went back to Stannaway Road, where Christy asked Lynch to take him to the toilet. He had not been shocked by Christy's appearance – he knew what to expect – but this took him aback. 'It was just so unusual, an experience I had never had before and do not expect to have again. Bear in mind the practicalities of having to hold up a man who couldn't stand, to do the unbuttoning, retrieval and aiming (things women don't have to think about), all in a very narrow space. All in all, it was a funny piece of business. Bear in mind, I wasn't, as the word "editor" might imply, a weighty intellectual but a twenty-year-old kid. I think, after meeting him, that Christy was a person of extraordinary talent and sensitivity, matched only in determination by his amazing mother.'

Christy was quite accustomed to getting strangers to take him to the toilet and was no longer embarrassed; in fact, by this time, it was quite a tradition. The Stone Boat welcomed him with open arms and most of the regular drinkers there knew that Christy needed help going to the Gents. As Mona remembered, a common joke in the Brown household at the time was 'Ah, sure, everyone in Kimmage has seen Christy's dick.' Lynch was uncomfortable helping Christy but he did the best he could. For him, it was worse not being able to understand what Christy was saying; he struggled to catch him and they could not really have a conversation. He was particularly struck by the way Christy was constantly grinding his teeth. *The Holy Door* published two of Christy's poems: 'Brendan', in the first edition, and 'Modern Idyll', in the third.

In April 1965, Dr Sheehan's husband, Bobby, died suddenly. All the Browns rallied around her as if 'they had lost one of their own'. At the funeral, on 30 April 1965, Sheehan went to have a word with Christy and thank him for coming. He handed her a letter, which, she later told the *Irish Times*, 'continued to sustain and comfort me . . . it shows a facet of his philosophy of life and his spirituality.' It reads:

My very Dear Friend,

I shall not quote clichés to you however excellent, however well intentioned; we are not the kind of friends who need clichés. You shall grieve the loss of your husband, your loved one, most privately and most intensely, and no one in all the world has the power to lessen that grief, or has the right to, not even for the love of you.

The very most we can try to do, we who care for you and love you in the limited human way we can love, is to keep you in the centre of our everyday consciousness; only then are we of any ultimate worth in the eyes of God and of man; to pray, within our limited capacity of prayer, that you may have the good grace and strength to survive and surmount this terrible cross, the most heartbreaking you will ever be called upon to bear, with the dignity, understanding and innate goodness of soul you possess. No one in the world can understand or share your sorrow; no facile words of comfort can alleviate your human pain. This is yours, and yours alone. Yours to live with, and yours to die with.

We, who care for your peace and love, the very wonderful person that is you, can only look on from the fringe of your life and hope for the ultimate best for you. There is much that I would wish for you; peace of mind, acceptance of whatever fate there is in life, the cheerful good-humoured tolerance of life that only comes from general understanding; all this I would wish for you in abundance, plus the love and admiration of those you are nearest to and hold dear. But all this is not had for the courage of wishing; all this you will earn only by your faith and courage, by the outward flow of your active love of life in helping others not gifted with your unique heart, your singular warmth of understanding; others not gifted by being you.

Your grief is your own, all the days of your life. Let no one deprive you of it, not even out of love. Pain is inseparable from love; that is a truth we must live with. It is a proof of our true inner reality, a judgement of ourselves, as to how and with what courage we face and accept that truth.

I am nothing, and because I know that, I am keenly aware of how inadequate and inarticulate my words must sound. They are not meant to comfort; only to reassure you that another shares your loss in his own inadequate way. You will not know comfort except in

Christy's first Holy Communion,
22 November 1939.

From left to right: Christy's mother, Bridget,
his sister Mona, Christy and Katriona
Maguire (née Delahunt).

Christy posing for the *Sunday Independent* newspaper after
winning a painting competition, 1944
(courtesy of the *Sunday Independent*).

Christy's father,
Patrick Brown, in 1954.

Dr Robert Collis
(courtesy of *La Vie Catholique*).

Bridget and Patrick at
Dublin airport, waiting
with Christy for the plane
to London.

Francis Brown transcribing for his brother in 1954. Christy is sitting in what the family nicknamed 'the electric chair'; the restraints were intended to control his muscle spasms and improve his posture.

Christy and his mother in the front window of 54 Stannaway Road, Kimmage, Dublin.

Christy and his brother Tony posing for the magazine *John Bull*, which serialised *My Left Foot* in 1954.

Brendan Behan's mother, Kathleen Behan, talking with Christy and his sister Ann Jones (courtesy of the National Library of Ireland).

Christy posing for the French magazine *La Vie Catholique* (courtesy of *La Vie Catholique*).

The Brown family at their mother's funeral, 8 August 1968. Back row from left: Francis, Peter, Tony, Peggy, Paddy, Jim, Seán, Eamonn; bottom row from left: Mona, Liz, Ann, Christy; sitting: Danny.

All the Brown brothers after Bridget's funeral. Back row from left: Francis, Jim, Uncle Peter, Danny, Seán, Paddy, Eamonn; front row from left: Tony, Christy, Peter.

Christy and Beth Moore sightseeing on the Staten Island Ferry, New York, 1960.

Christy swimming and steering the Moores' boat in Connecticut, 1960.

Beth and Deac Moore, Christy and Seán
in County Wicklow, 1965.

Christy and Seán on holiday in America, 1970. Christy and Beth were
arguing, so the brothers went to stay with a local couple whom they
had befriended (the woman is pictured to the right). Later, Christy would
write as a dedication on the back of the painting, 'To Seán, for
enduring that long hot summer so gracefully.'

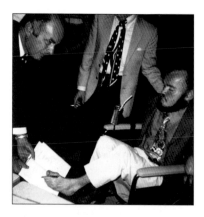

Christy signing books in
America after the publication of
Down All the Days in 1970.

A portrait of Christy by the Irish
photographer Fergus Bourke.

Christy and Ann (far left) meeting journalists and photographers at their
shared home, Lisheen, in Rathcoole, 1971.

Posing for a photographer from *Paris Match in* 1971, Ann holds a copy
of the bestselling *Down All the Days* so that Christy can sign it
(courtesy of *Paris Match*).

Christy in the Stone Boat, Kimmage,
with his brother-in-law Willy Jones (courtesy of the *Irish Times*).

Christy on his wedding day, 5 October 1972, leaving the registry office in Kildare Street, Dublin. Seán is pushing Christy's wheelchair. Christy's wife, Mary, is behind Seán's left shoulder, standing next to Ann. Noel Pearson, Christy's friend and producer of the film of *My Left Foot*, stands just behind Seán (courtesy of the *Irish Independent*).

Christy and Mary at the reception, organised by Noel Pearson and held at Sutton House Hotel, near Howth, on the County Dublin coast (courtesy of the *Irish Independent*).

Christy and Mary in
County Kerry, 1975.

Christy at Seán's flat in London
with Kelvin Moyses (Seán's
partner). The photograph was
taken in May 1981, five months
before Christy's death.

Christy's funeral at Glasnevin Cemetery, Dublin, 14 September 1981.
From left to right: Wille O'Donnell, Mary Brown, Peggy Barclay,
Darren Jones, Kelvin Moyses (courtesy of the *Irish Times*).

The Brown family on the set of *My Left Foot*, working as extras.
Top row from left: Francis, Paddy, Willy, Eamonn, Tom;
bottom row from left: Mona, Ann, Kay, Betty
(courtesy of Ferndale Films).

At the premiere of *My Left Foot*: (left to right) Ann Jones,
Daniel Day-Lewis, Mona Byrne, Peggy Barclay, Seán Brown
(courtesy of the *Irish Times*).

A sketch drawn by Christy in 1965. His brother Francis believes this is how Christy imagined himself if he had had the use of all his limbs – playing an instrument.

A pencil drawing entitled *The Resurrection* (1958).

These sketches are copies
from the Austrian artist
Egon Schiele's nudes.

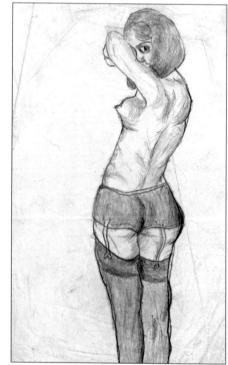

A painting of a character who appears in *Down All the Days*. 'Red Magso', as Christy called her in his novel, was one of his mother's close friends and lived on Ferns Road in Kimmage.

A possible self-portrait (1969). The painting bears a striking resemblance to Vincent van Gogh's self-portraits.

Three still life paintings created for the Disabled Artists Association.

your own heart, in the knowledge that you have shared the best years of your life with a good man, who loved you, and who you loved with a love that will never quite be lost – to either of you.

God Bless and love you,
Chris

In the autumn of 1965, Christy wrote to Patricia and Katriona, and he was panicked: Beth and Deac Moore were doing a European tour and were coming to Dublin for five days. Christy invited them to stay and promised them he would take them sightseeing, suggesting they visit a 'real Irish pub' amongst other things. Ann remembers how Deac Moore, a huge American man with a drawling American accent, walked into 54 Stannaway Road and declared, 'Gee, I *love* your little cottage!' The Browns tried to explain that it wasn't a cottage, it was their house but Deac did not understand. The Moores met Mona, Ann and Katriona, took tours around the Wicklow countryside and went to the local pub. When Beth left, Christy was heartbroken again. After five years, since his first visit to see Beth in 1960, nothing had changed. He wrote:

> I knew the love would still be there, that can never alter. But it is one thing to love, it is quite another to want. And that is what surprised me, dismayed me, tormented and delighted me – that we should still want each other, not just as much, but more than ever. I had so dulled myself with alcohol and secondary emotions over the past five years that I thought I could meet her again and remain intact, immune; how damn wrong you can be!

After the visit, Beth invited Christy to come and stay with them in Connecticut again. Her arrival and quick departure left him depressed. He stayed in his study drinking, writing and listening to his favourite pieces of music: *Madame Butterfly*, *Tosca*, *Aida*, *La Bohème* and anything by Gilbert and Sullivan.

Chapter Nine

AN ARTIST

As you have most probably guessed by now, since this is Saturday and
since the kitty is not entirely dry, I am not entirely sober, thanks
be to Jasus, hence the somewhat erratic typography, for which again
I apologise. It merely goes to show, doesn't it, that I am as much
of a fucking bore in print when "under" as I am face to face under
similar circumstances. Jesus, it's like the fucking Battle of the
Boyne looking back over this page with so many printing casualties.
I must seriously consider employing a secretary to work under me...
"under me" being the operative phrase.
Well, what the hell can I say to you that wouldn't be better said
over a pint?   (O Christ- I really do apologise for the really awful
typing, mate.) All the usual old things come to mind- like, I hope
you're keeping well and look after yourself and keep working for the
good of your health at least and don't be fucking too much and write
home now and then and don't forget your dear old Mother far across the
sea and say your fucking prayers every night and always remember you
are a fucking Irishman and an even more fucking Catholic and God bless
Ireland says the hero trying-to knock twopence off the latest price
of Willie Reilly's black-and-white-minstrel pudding, and Father
Charles's grave is still venerated regularly every other ecumenical
Sunday by the sundry devout and fervent ones may God bless their
naively unecumenical souls. Ah yes, methinks my typing is getting
oh so gradually better.

As you have most probably guessed by now, since this is Saturday and since the kitty is not entirely dry, I am not entirely sober, thanks be to Jasus, hence the somewhat erratic typography, for which again I apologise. It merely goes to show, doesn't it, that I am as much of a fucking bore in print when 'under' as I am face to face under similar circumstances. Jesus, it's like the fucking Battle of the Boyne looking back over these pages with so many printing casualties. I must seriously consider employing a secretary to work under me . . . 'under me' being the operative phrase.

Well, what the hell can I say to you that wouldn't be better said over a pint? (O Christ – I really do apologise for the really awful typing, mate). All the usual old things come to mind – like, I hope you're keeping well and look after yourself and keep working for the good of your health at least and don't be fucking too much and write home now and then and don't forget your dear old Mother far across the sea and say your fucking prayers every night and always remember you are a fucking Irishman and an even more fucking Catholic and God bless Ireland says the hero trying to knock twopence off the latent price of Willie Reilly's black-and-white minstrel pudding, and Father Charles's grave is still venerated regularly every other ecumenical Sunday by the sundry devout and fervent ones may God bless their naively unecumenical souls. Ah yes, methinks my typing is getting oh so gradually better.

Christy Brown, writing to his brother Seán,
5 February 1967

At the end of 1967, Christy wished his kitty fuller. Although it was probably a rare instance that he had extra money, it would not be rare that whatever he could find he would spend on drinking at home or more likely in his local pubs, the Stone Boat and the Four Roads in Kimmage. He had spent quite a bit of money travelling to America to see Beth Moore again;

he stayed with her in upstate New York for three months. In February 1967, Christy went to Stamford, Connecticut, a third time to stay with Beth, her husband and their three children (he became quite fond of their youngest daughter, Margaret, writing a poem of the same name for her).

The weather was superb when he arrived. He went sailing with Deac and Beth on the Long Island Sound and the Connecticut River and thought that 'if he ever got rich' he would buy himself a boat and sail around the coast of Dublin. He went to lectures, theatres and concerts in New York City and visited Boston. Christy particularly loved the sense of history he felt when he visited the town of Concord in Massachusetts, where the American Revolution began. What he loved most was seeing the whimsical and delicate Christmas lights on display in Hartford, Connecticut – that and spending time on his own with Beth.

It would be Beth to whom Christy would dedicate *Down All the Days*: 'For Beth, who with such gentle ferocity whipped me into finishing this book . . .' Beth had control over him. As his mother had been able to do when he was a boy, she tamed the wild Christy. He wrote to Seán saying that he was not allowed a drink in her home until he had finished an afternoon of writing – drinks were at 6 p.m. Beth told the *Stamford Advocate* in an interview in 1970: 'Every day I told him he had to do twenty pages or he wouldn't get his gargle.'

Christy and Beth went to New York City together and in Greenwich Village they met the artist Peter Lipman-Wulf, who made a bronze cast of Christy. They went to what he describes in one of his letters as 'the play to see', Tom Stoppard's *Rosencrantz and Guildenstern Are Dead*, which had just opened on Broadway. As time went on, Christy's feelings for Beth remained the same. As he watched the summer season end and autumn begin, he felt contented. He felt comfortable with the Moores, not only because he had visited them before but also because his first stay had been such a happy, even a liberating, experience – and he was deeply in love.

During the trip, he also met the poet Raymond Roseliep, probably the most widely published haiku poet in North America. They found they had an affinity for the same metaphysical questions and, of course, a love of poetry. Roseliep was a Catholic priest as well as a poet. He was born in Iowa and spent most of his life in Dubuque, with the exception of his seminary studies, undertaken at the Catholic University of America in Washington DC. In the 1960s, he began to experiment with concrete poetry and his most notable works were published in the '70s.

Roseliep gave Christy a copy of his just released book of poems, which they both signed. Roseliep wrote, 'To Christy Brown from his brother bardic spirit. Hail to thee Chris.' On the title page, Christy inscribed under the title, *Love Makes the Air Light*, 'YES! Chris Brown. Conn. USA.' In the letters they exchanged later, Roseliep sent Christy a haiku:

> Christy wrote me with
> His left toes. I'm sure of clouds
> now, less sure of me.

Their letters discuss Picasso and Van Gogh and whether or not God exists and why Christy suffered from his infirmity. Roseliep wrote telling him that Picasso had said, 'He that loves God cannot expect to be loved by God in return.' Christy thought this was a terrible but powerful aphorism, with some 'grain of truth' in it. Given Roseliep's vocation, it is unsurprising that they wrote a great deal about the meaning of life. Christy found Roseliep's hope and faith charming but naive. For Christy, virtue seemed 'but an excuse to be sanctimonious and hypocritical'; he did not 'visualise an entirely amoral world, nor even an honest to goodness immoral one', but to him there was 'an intolerable absence of free air and space in our modern religious code'. While reading St Augustine's *Confessions*, he wrote that it was 'while experiencing our life search that we must think and probe and search in ourselves if we are to understand anything at all. Each fact helps to build a conviction, each conviction helps to build faith, and faith is the only thing that gives human life any meaning or value.'

His faith was being tested in his work. Having published only five poems since *My Left Foot*, Christy's sole income was from his work with the Disabled Artists Association and his plays and poetry were failing to create a niche for him in the writing world of Dublin. Yet, as one can read in the letter at the start of this chapter, his sense of humour remained intact, as did his aspirations to write another book, which he told Katriona Maguire he had 'to get out of his system'. He wrote to tell her that he was working on something that was

> about Dublin working-class life as I know it, with no great plot or even melodramatic situations. It depends ultimately upon its relation to life and its concern with the truth of that life. It is hard, demanding work . . . it will take another year or so to get finished.
>
> I regard it as the acid test as to whether I am a writer in the real sense of the word.

No one was expecting him to write a novel as controversial and as lyrical as what he produced. Just like himself, his second book would be harsh, cruel and brutally honest but balanced with an intense sensitivity. This juxtaposition of the grim and the romantic was not merely a technique; it was part of his nature.

His visit to America cheered him up enormously; however, it also evoked one of his bouts of depression, just as it had done in 1960. Upon returning, he again missed Beth, and the freedom that America allowed him. In Ireland, it was back to the grindstone with the Disabled Artists Association, which Christy had begun to despise. His art was never the issue, he felt; rather, it was his performance – and after years and years, the routine had become incredibly tiresome. Not only was the DAA treating him poorly but the work was proving too much for Christy. However, he stuck with it because it was hard to find another way of earning money. He hated the hypocrisy of Irish society and he knew very well how preposterous notions of charity and kindness were when they came from an oppressive Church.

Christy was in a treacherous corner. The DAA's exhibition tours meant he had to travel for hours over long distances in the countryside to paint in odd places. It tired him and humiliated him and the pay was not very good. He vented his anger in the best way he knew how. He wrote to the DAA time and time again complaining that his brothers were taking him to these places and no one was paying the expenses. Despite Seán Feehan's having published a paperback edition of *My Left Foot*, Christy's attitude towards him had soured. What's more, his pay was not that of a fully fledged member of the association. He wrote to Katriona telling her:

> I think you are absolutely right to think that I am being treated in a very off-hand manner by the DAA. Apart from what they pay me, which after all isn't much, nobody shows the least bit of interest in what I am doing. The trouble is, there isn't very much anybody can do; the few protests I made were peremptorily dismissed by Feehan and were treated as impertinent threats. Herr Stegmann, the boss, is practically unreachable, except through Feehan, and needless to say, there is no sense in trying to reach him that way. I ought to have qualified a long time ago now as a full member and be paid a full salary; I think my work qualifies as such, but for some reason or other, or perhaps merely through indifference, I am being kept back. My most recent work does not get through to Stegmann, who I am sure would put it before the committee for approval of my full membership, which is how they do things. It is all very frustrating,

I get my monthly cheque, yes, £22.10.0, which works out at around £5.5 or so each week; out of this I pay my mother my keep, buy materials and anything else that crops up, and try to have a little pocket money occasionally.

Christy asked the DAA in Cork what he would have to do to be paid better and work in better conditions. Stifled and stiff replies came from them, so he decided to write to the director of the institute in Germany, Erich Stegmann. Stegmann came to meet Christy in Kimmage in March 1967. Stegmann (who had no arms and painted with his mouth) was like Christy in that he enjoyed a drink. At 54 Stannaway Road, Stegmann and Christy knocked back whiskeys together. Christy, of course, used a straw and Stegmann placed his drink on top of the fireplace, next to an ashtray with his cigarette in it. He would pick up the glass with his teeth, knock back a shot and then grab the cigarette with his lips, take a drag and place it back in the ashtray. Christy lay on the floor or sat sipping his drink while the two of them listened to music and Christy's left foot swung back and forth to the rhythm as always. After meeting Stegmann, Christy was so fond of him that he invited him to stay in the Brown family home for the rest of his time in Dublin, and Stegmann accepted. After that, Christy was made a full member of the DAA and his income was increased.

The DAA were not the only people who received what might be euphemistically described as aggressive letters; banks, lawyers and others also received letters in which Christy would complain about the late arrival of his pay cheques from Germany and the lack of credit he was being given. The situation with his former friend and driver did not help matters either. He had borrowed £1,000 from a bank in Dublin, with Christy as guarantor. The driver had failed to make repayments, so Christy was left to foot the bill. His mother was working at the time and one can imagine that this debt and his inability to help with the finances at home would have sent Christy wild. He adored Bridget and would do anything for her. So he wrote and complained and sought out writers and artists in Dublin who might help him pursue his dream of publishing his work.

His worry about his inability to provide for Bridget is echoed in a letter he wrote to Katriona. Brendan Behan had died on 20 March 1964 and Christy complained to her about Dominic Behan, his brother (also a writer), and how

> sad it is that a fine old woman like Kathleen Behan should be left in near penury now at the end of her full and varied life. It is terrible that she should now be dependent for a roof over her head on some of Brendan's literary friends and admirers. Dominic must be a complete bastard to neglect her like this. God knows he's earning enough money now to buy his mother a little house ten times over. I always admired him as a writer, but never much as a man. Not long before I went to America, I had an unfortunate run-in with him in my 'Local', when he came in drunk one night and sat at our table and started systematically to insult me and denigrate my work. It isn't easy to treat a bloke with contempt when he's obviously below contempt and your own blood is at boiling point, but anyway he came out of the skirmish considerably worse for wear and with even less dignity than he'd had at the start. But, I'd forgive him all his many slips if he'd look after his mother and treat her with half the grace and respect of Brendan. Brothers and writers they may be – but there the similarity ends as far as I am concerned.

Apart from the wishing to be able to protect his mother, whose health was slowly deteriorating, Christy was also desperate to make more money so that he could see more of Beth.

By mid-1967, he was tired of reading about other great writers and their successes – writers who had been published in the same periodicals as him. He envied and adored other poets who were successful. As Katriona remembers it, he had a 'love–hate relationship' with Patrick Kavanagh (he had once shown Kavanagh one of his poems and his reply was dismissive and rude). Christy would always complain about Kavanagh and his work but in a letter to Katriona Maguire, written after the poet's death on 30 November 1967, Christy told her:

> I do not know if Kavanagh was a genius, nor do I care. I do not know if Behan was a genius, and care less. I happen to admire most of what they did, each in their own fashion, and only incidentally acknowledge the real or transitory contribution they each made to Irish literature . . . if, as that article you sent me said, Kavanagh knew he was immortal, then no wonder at times he was such an impossible man, such an embittered man, for God knows it is hard enough to bear the thought of one's own mortality without being burdened by the awareness of one's immortality, in spirit if not in flesh. I always write best myself with the comforting thought – almost the certainty – that what I am writing today will not be remembered or even read tomorrow; the possibility that it might live on would be a serious inhibition to any daring or originality I might possess. Anyway, I hope his bones rest easy tonight wherever they might lie. In a way, a good poet never dies, and that is something to be thankful for. That is why I cannot agree with you that the Irish literary scene is nearly dead just because most of its leading lights are now in the clay . . . there is a whole new generation of new Irish poets, writers and playwrights rapidly emerging and some of whom have indeed already emerged in splendid colours and with talent enough to keep the Parnassian torch flaming for many a day to come. There is Brian Moore from Belfast writing his brilliant sharp brooding novels of industrial Irish life; the ubiquitous, controversial, inimitable Edna O'Brien, who has yet I think to be fully appreciated as a writer of people and not merely what people do; Eugene McCabe, who is ready to assume the

mantle of the premier dramatist of Ireland and who is almost Ibsen-like in his analysis of rural and country life; Brian Friel, who is still of course young enough to be the vanguard of this maturing generation of writers and whose comical bittersweet plays are good enough to enthrall an international audience. Among the poets I could call many to mind . . . John Montague, Brendan Kennelly, Tom Kinsella . . . James Liddy, Brian Lynch . . . Michael Hartnett . . . from the bones of the dead come flowers, and out of the defeated dust of Ireland some men who are alive and unafraid to record and celebrate that fact.

After writing this letter, Christy composed a poem that he entitled 'A Kind of Lament for Patrick Kavanagh'. He writes of Kavanagh as a kind of lord in the poetic world of Dublin (which, he notes, was never his city), haughty and supercilious. 'Were you magnanimous?' he asks. Not to me in my 'beardless years', he answers, although he notes that 'on a rare day' the poet would even suffer fools 'who put whiskey in expecting wisdom to come out'. Christy uses the symbol of the hawk for Kavanagh, a compliment of sorts, because the hawk in Christy's work always indicates knowledge of the tragedy that is about to fall upon all the characters in whatever situation his poetry or prose finds itself. He writes of Kavanagh both as 'monarch and messiah of McDaid's' (a Dublin pub famous for its literary clientele) and alone, walking the canal banks 'stopping to be a child again with children / emptying the gems of your unhoared treasure / under that dense derogatory sky'. When Christy heard the news of Kavanagh's passing, he says, he was on the 'contrary side of the moon' and 'saw a shooting star' – but he 'called it mere coincidence'. A joke, and a compliment, which Kavanagh could well have appreciated.

This poem as much as any other tells us about who Christy Brown was as a person; both he and Kavanagh knew the pains of alcoholism and the effort required to survive as a professional writer.

As Anthony Cronin remembers in his memoir of Dublin literary life, *Dead as Doornails*, Kavanagh, the formidable intellect and great man, was in his last days left to sleeping with a bottle of whiskey under the pillow of his bed, which he had to reach for every time he woke or indeed moved. Christy knew where this pain came from; he knew he was an alcoholic and he says it time and time again in his letters. Of course, he was self-conscious and his notion of being on stage all the time can hardly be questioned. Likewise, himself, Kavanagh and Behan all suffered from the stereotypical image foisted on them by the media – that of a drunk Irishman on stage, offering sage words for the literary devout, come to supply free drink – an image that actually killed the work, or rather killed the artist. Like Behan, who used profanity on the BBC for the first time, Christy would do the same on RTÉ.

Christy Brown had a fervour for living which was unbelievable. As Noel Pearson (Christy's agent and friend, who would later produce the film *My Left Foot*) remembers, Christy used to try to jump out of his wheelchair onto passing buses in Dublin, with no fear of damaging himself. Fear was not a friend to him; sitting and waiting for things to happen was not an option. Bravery was something Christy admired and he stuck to a lifelong policy of indifference to what anyone thought of him. Still, the sensitive side of his character was being torn apart by the treatment he was receiving from the Disabled Artists Association. What is more, his last published major work, *My Left Foot*, was by this time an embarrassment to him. This, he believed in his heart of hearts, was not literature. It was a miracle story of a miracle boy who had survived against all the odds – a mawkish tale. The idea that *My Left Foot* was what he would be remembered for haunted him and he was crying out to be recognised as a writer of other things. It is clear, when

Christy writes about Behan and Kavanagh, that he deeply understands their circumstances but also that, by 1968, he feels they have had their day and that his turn is coming. He had worked long and hard on his new novel, and continued to work on it, and he was excited about the prospect that it might in the end be a masterpiece.

His paintings reflect this desire to grow as an artist. In the early 1960s, he produced still lifes, religious scenes, flowers in vases and pictures of Dublin streetscapes covered in snow and rain. As the decade progressed, so did his work and the canvasses became deeper, mostly portraits of himself or of people he knew – people who, like him, lived in stages of frenzy and inspiration coupled with frustration and anger. His portrait of Brendan Behan shows in its distorted shaping and subdued earth tones a sad and private individual, distant from the viewer. Likewise, Christy's self-portraits often combine his own image with that of Christ weeping or bleeding. Once, his sister Ann asked him about one of these self-portraits. 'Is that Jesus or you?' she enquired. 'Both,' he said simply, and stared at the painting.

One of his most telling paintings is of 'Red Magso', who lived on Ferns Road in Kimmage and often called at Stannaway Road or paused with Bridget at the local shop or on a street corner to have a gossip when Christy was out with his mother. Magso was one of the local characters; everyone in Kimmage would have known her or at least known of her. Three years after he finished the painting, Magso would be immortalised as one of the wildest characters in *Down All the Days*. Her breasts flop out of her blouse, as she drinks and drinks, making everyone around her laugh as she gives out about her late husband, who so loved her breasts, who filled her with babies from the first day of their marriage and who also never stopped drinking. Although Magso is genuinely hilarious in her repartee, she is also as tragic as any character can be. Her wit and constant quips are some of the best one-liners in the book. At one point, as she listens to the incessant playing of a horn by one of her neighbours, she says to another character, Old Essie, 'First thing in the morning he's at it, blowing that thing like Saint Gabriel himself . . .' Essie replies, 'And you don't know who he is, you say?'

'Sure if I knew that,' Magso says, 'I'd give him a different kind of horn to think about.'

But like so many women in Dublin in the 1940s (when the book is set), Magso is trapped. Life has offered her only a marriage she could never leave, children and hard work. In the book, she is wild, rude and bold. In Christy's painting, she resembles Degas' bathers. Her back is turned to the viewer so we can see only a woman seated on a bed with her bra straps hanging off her shoulders. Her shoulders are slumped and her hair hangs loose, uncombed and unkempt, as she stares at her reflection in a large mirror hanging across from her bed. It is a delicate, feminine frame and the painting's use of soft blues and greys does not suggest a brash, wild woman; instead, Christy shows he knows the internal pain Magso has.

It was that way that a new artist was emerging. Christy's hatred of sympathy, of being on display and of acting as a puppet on whom other people could project themselves was intensifying and these ideas were now starting to show in his work. His images were becoming deeper, his thoughts more malicious and scathing, and a book was forming inside him that would display all the lies life and people told and all the pain Dublin people felt, that would change him from 'the writer of *My Left Foot*' to simply a writer.

Christy often wrote to his younger brother Seán in the early hours of the morning after he had taken quite a few drinks and his tone is usually informal and intimate. None of the pedantic language he uses when writing to Katriona Maguire is found in his letters to Seán and anyone reading the correspondence can tell the two brothers shared a lot – and trusted one another – in their adversities, opinions and laughter. To find Christy the artist, his letters to Seán Brown may well be the best place to begin. To Seán, he wrote about how all people lead two different lives – the external and the internal. He felt we should all share at least part of our lives with each other, before we get 'too old and selfish to share anything at all'. It is said that all artists paint themselves. What, then, did Christy think of art? And what therefore did he think of himself? He knew people thought to themselves 'He did that? With his left foot?', instead of simply looking at his work.

But Christy was prepared to share a part of himself; in fact, he was adamant that he would. Women who wrote to him would receive a reply from a man who would pour out his heart to virtual strangers, and his poetry opens wounds which echo the most private parts of his pain. Privacy was not a friend of Christy's. As Shane Connaughton (who wrote the screenplay for *My Left Foot* and who met Christy when he performed in a stage adaptation of *Down All the Days* in Dublin in 1981) puts it, 'From the moment he was born, he was given a double life sentence, Christy. We all get one life sentence but he got two. The key was thrown away on him. "There you are, Christy: you're jailed in your own body for the rest of your life." Can you imagine that sentence?'

This image of a prison was what inspired Connaughton to have Daniel Day-Lewis as Christy in the film, when asked what he thought of Hamlet, answer simply: 'A cripple.' Christy saw poverty lock his family and himself, especially his father, in a social jail cell; his physical disability, his second level of imprisonment, would have led him to see the very best and the very worst of people's characters. Many people must wonder, dear God, how did he go on? How could he keep on living? Christy did ask this question himself and during his darkest depressions, he would consider suicide. All his characters, whether in painting, prose or poems, echo the difficulty of living; he understands how terrifying it is for everyone simply to exist. As he wrote in November 1968:

As I say, I'm working away and deriving some pleasure from it. After all, I'm getting paid good money, even if I don't seem to be able to do much with it, and I have to show a fair return. At certain stages in our lives everything seems pointless, meaningless, without purpose; we think we can't possibly endure another day without going insane. Yet, somehow life goes on. We survive to face another battle. And if we're lucky, we not only survive, but we actually start to live again, to find life not completely dark and empty but alive again with possibilities and fresh interests. The power to overcome despair and the will to go on living seem to come from outside of ourselves. We discover once more how difficult it is to really reject life. Our hearts get broken every day we live, in one way or another, yet we learn somehow to live with it. I don't presume to understand many things. I am as lost and as ignorant and as desperate as the next man, but I think I have begun to realise life must be lived for its own sake and not merely be used as a vessel or an outlet for our own desires and ambitions. There is something in the best and worst of us that drives us on past despair itself and to a kind of gradual peace, a peace not merely of mind but of spirit, a peace that might well be the beginning of real wisdom.

By wisdom, I do not mean the purely mental or intellectual kind, I do not mean mere cleverness or brilliance, but rather the capacity to see beyond the narrow boundaries of our everyday existence to something we can only one day hope to know and attain. What that something is God only knows. Maybe heaven and eternity and all the rest of it is merely one unending process of getting nearer and nearer to the truth of ourselves, and therefore nearer to that something which we, under many different names, call God.

I am just trying to find things out for myself, to get myself organised and get all the pictures that I think I have in my head out into colour, and all the poems I have in there out into print. I know of no other way to

live. I only know that you are either in life or out of it.
You cannot pretend to be alive and not dare to live. The
only real horror that I could ever know would be to think
that I have learnt nothing at all from my mother's life and
death.

For, on 8 August 1968, Bridget Brown had suffered a heart
attack. She was taken to Meath Hospital in Dublin for emergency
surgery. She was there for only three days and late on the third
night, she died. Although her health had been getting worse
for many years, her death was a shock to Christy's system and
in some ways he would never recover. At the funeral he said
nothing. A few days afterwards, the local priest came around
to the family home and asked to speak to Christy. Christy said
he wanted nothing more to do with the Church and he told
the priest, as clearly as he could, to 'fuck off'. His sister Ann
was appalled and concerned that she, her husband and Christy
would all be excommunicated. She tried to speak to him about
the problem, telling him he could at least apologise and make
amends, but Christy would have none of it. He told her he
had only given the Church and its rituals respect because of
his mother's faith. Now that she had passed on, there was
no point in doing so ever again. Ann remembers, 'She had a
hard life. I mean, I was only twenty-four when Mammy died.
I remember when she died, I didn't believe she was going to
die but she said, "Ann, promise me now, if anything happens
to me, promise me you will take care of Christy." She died the
next day. She knew.'

His family remember Christy as inconsolable; he would
speak to no one. He was plunged into the worst depression he
would ever suffer. Christy would not eat and began drinking
even more; his weight dropped to an alarmingly low level. His
late sister Mona remembered that the family were seriously
worried about him: he would do nothing but lie on the couch
in the family home, staring at the wall or sleeping. The only
person who could really get through to him in any way was his

younger sister Ann. The two had always been close but after his mother died, as Ulick O'Connor says, 'Ann really was Christy's girl, in a way, because she was so good to him.' Ann completely took over Bridget's role as Christy's carer and dedicated herself to looking after him exactly as his mother had for thirty-six years. While she took care of her two young children, she and her husband Willy shared a home with Christy and helped him with all his physical needs as well as his psychological ones. Like Bridget, she would attempt to curtail his drinking and when he needed to get in touch with anyone – his publishers or friends – Ann always helped him. As Noel Pearson says, 'I think the heroes of the whole piece are his mother and his sister Ann. She was really good, she was really the best. I think she nursed him more than any of the rest. I mean, they all loved him but she lived with him. She was terrific to him, you know.'

Her commitment to him and the hard work it entailed was such that Christy would dedicate his first, beloved collection of poetry, *Come Softly to My Wake* (1971), to her. He wrote: 'For Ann, for helping to keep the ship afloat.' Christy knew that without her help and protection, he might very well have sunk into an oblivion of drink and depression that could have killed him.

After Bridget's death, Christy immersed himself in work, finding escape in the writing of his novel. By January 1969, he had completed *Down All the Days*; he had used all the pain, anguish and memories he had. It was finished. He sent the book to David Farrer, his editor at Secker & Warburg. Still, he was desperately unhappy. He was confident about the book he had finally written, but as he told Seán in 1969:

> Amazingly, at a time when life promises so much for me I feel very depressed and despondent, for no particular reason, just a combination of circumstances, I guess. I have so much to live for, especially now that I have the novel done and financially things will get better, yet I feel so bloody unhappy within myself. I'm reasonably

sure it isn't just sexual deprivation that is the trouble; I think I am fairly in control of the perennial aspect of my existence by now. Unhappily I think it goes deeper. I am a very disappointed man in some ways. Disappointed about myself and disappointed about other people. I have grown accustomed to being disappointed with myself, being disappointed with other people is something else again. I realise it is the height of folly to expect more of people than they can honestly give, but unfortunately, I seem to do this all the time, with the inevitable result that I'm left with a feeling of bitterness and anger, more with myself than with those concerned. I seem to learn so little as time goes by. The sum total of my 37 years on earth seems merely to be one continuous record of my optimism continually cancelled out by defeat. I seem to have wasted so much of myself in mean sordid ways, wasted so much of the love and loyalty I might have felt for other people, real people instead of the shadowy people who seemed to have filled my life. Looking back from what feels to be an incredibly long period of mortality, the only real people in my life seem to have been my mother, most of all mother . . . and my father, whom I never loved and often hated, but who nonetheless was a very real person indeed and a very honest person in his own right. He was a bastard by every decent standard, but at least he was honest about it, maybe because he wasn't clever enough to be dishonest about it, but you at least knew what to expect from him.

And of course, I do not have to tell you that the most real and important person in my life after my mother has always been Beth Moore. I love her, and what is more amazing is she loves me. Which just shows you how the most intelligent people can be so lamentably wrong at times, but there you have it. And yet even with her I feel a million light years away at times. I love her, as I say, but love seems incapable sometimes of bridging that terrific gulf between us. It all seems so remote from the everyday life that I have to live here. Sometimes, as true as God, I forget that I ever touched her, it becomes so hard to remember what it was like. This may not strike you as the ideal description of love but it is at least true. And so I go through my life, trying to avoid shadows, like any other man, I suppose, standing and trying to survive in my own little truth. And of course, I am weak, terribly weak, and I give way, and it all becomes too much for me, and I take the coward's way out and I get pissing blind drunk too often for my own good. And I feel shame afterwards but most of all I feel frustration and despair and a bitter sense of time passing. I know all this is depressing, and I'm sorry, but I felt I had to talk to someone just now . . . .

God Bless you and keep a sup for me.

Chris

Chapter Ten

AN INTERNATIONAL BESTSELLER

I had a letter today from David Farrer and he is absolutely convinced this book is going to be something of a literary earthquake and is absolutely confident of its future. He really thinks it is going to hit the world straight between the eyes. I go one better than that. I think it will hit the world slap-bang between the bollacks.

I had such a horrible fear, all these years, that I was a literary freak, a one-book man, a real literary flash-in-the-pan. I knew the bloody thing was there, the talent, the urge, the hellish genius, whatever you like to call it; I knew it was there, inside me. Like a trapped animal. But how the hell was I going to get it out, set it free, release it upon an unsuspecting world? For years, I lived with this dilemma, for years I lived in the shadow of my first book, in the shadow of Bob Collis, the man who helped me shape that damn book and who many people thought was the author of that damn book. The rest of the world does not know the grinding labour that went into the writing of that little book, but you do Seán, because you were one of the 'hands' in the writing of it, and you know the hell I went through in writing that book. It is all so very different this time. I have been completely on my own in this, and sometimes I have cried bitterly alone in bed at night at what I considered my own dismal lack of talent. God knows it is not modesty that makes me say this, but I really never thought I would write another book . . . I am more than a little over-awed, Seán, by my own achievement, and I say this in full knowledge of my own inadequacy and lack of talent.

Goddamit, this machine isn't going too well, and for a £200 investment I would expect better things. Goddamn this superlative all-modern typewriter. I'd do better with a pencil stuck between my toes.

God Bless you Seán. I feel happy now that I'll be seeing you soon. Keep faith in yourself, and nothing can ever really go wrong.

Christy Brown, writing to his brother Seán,
September 1969

David Farrer was worried when he received the manuscript of *Down All the Days* in late 1969. He dreaded that he might have to tell Christy that the work was not up to scratch. But instead of finding a book that was not even close to being publishable, what he discovered amazed him. He felt instantly that he was reading a landmark piece of literature. He worried that some parts of the book went on for far too long but he thought he could edit the text down to a reasonable size. Christy, he told the writer John Banville, had written a superb novel.

Banville first met David Farrer in 1963, when he sent his first book to four or five publishers and Farrer was the one who accepted it. He regards Farrer as one of 'the last of his kind of literary editors'. As he says, '[Farrer] was the last of that type . . . During the war, he was private secretary to Lord Beaverbrook. He said to me once, "You know, on my first job I used to go to work on an elephant." I said, "What?" He said, "Oh, yes, I was tutor to an Indian prince, and the elephant would come round for me at nine o'clock every morning." He was one of those closet gays. That is, he didn't mention that he was gay. In those days the word hadn't been invented. He came to Dublin and took my wife and me to dinner at the old Russell Hotel on St Stephen's Green. He had this man with him, his partner, I presume, and we finally realised David was gay. In those days, we assumed that everybody was heterosexual, and I'd assumed that David was. But David was part of that 1930s, '40s, '50s world in England, where you didn't talk about these things.'

Banville believes that Farrer recognised something in Christy Brown, even though he was from a public-school, middle-class world and Christy was from the antithesis, that they were linked by their understanding of feeling outcast and knowing what it was to be an outsider. Farrer also had a knack for spotting a book that would be well received. Once, Banville and he went out to lunch together and Farrer told him that Secker & Warburg were publishing a book called *The History Man* (by Malcolm Bradbury) and that it 'really was quite good'. Banville asked, 'Good in what way?' and Farrer asked him what he meant. Banville said, 'Well, is it a literary book or . . . ?' and Farrer simply stared at him. After a brief moment, he replied, 'Well, it's just good.' And of course it was a huge success.

Farrer worked on several of Banville's books: 'As I say, David was the last of his particular kind of editor. I had a couple of editors after him who were superb, but David didn't really do technical editing. I remember with my second novel, *Birchwood*, I went to see David about it. I went into his office at eleven o'clock in the morning and he said, 'It's really very good. I think it will do very well.' In those days, when the book was published, you got back the typescript from the printers. When the script of *Birchwood* came, I saw that David's editing consisted of one small mark on the first page. I think he really hadn't read the rest of the book. He just thought, 'Yes, this will do.' You have to realise that in those days, fiction really was not sexy. I mean, it was really a poor man's business. Fiction didn't become fashionable until the 1980s, when the Booker Prize took off.'

After Farrer gave Banville a copy of *Down All the Days* in April 1970, he was moved enough to write to Christy:

Dear Mr Brown,

David Farrer has for so long been telling me how brilliant your book is that when a pre-publication copy arrived yesterday I must admit that I opened it nervously, expecting the worst; high praise has an unfortunate knack of producing, in me at least, all the ingredients of a hearty revulsion towards the thing praised. However, now that I have read *Down All the Days* I find that it is in my opinion an extraordinary and beautiful book . . . Certainly chapter sixteen is the loveliest piece of prose I've seen in a long time. I hope my enthusiasm is not making all this seem insincere; I've never written before now to any writer in praise of his work, and I find it difficult to do. Anyway, let me just say that I think *Down All the Days* is a brilliant book, one that perhaps will help Irish writing get away from the dire cabbage it seems to produce over and over again these days.

I shall be at your party in the Bailey on May 11, but I thought it wise to get in a small word of congratulations before all the big guns begin booming twenty-one gun salutes at you.

Good luck,

John Banville

Banville remembers the launch of *Down All the Days* as 'the craziest party I have ever been to'. He picked Farrer up from the airport and took him back to his house in the village of Howth at the end of Dublin Bay. At eleven in the morning, Banville was pleased he could offer Farrer a glass of whiskey (he and his wife had not much money at the time and had carefully selected the bottle). As Banville poured the drink, he watched and waited for Farrer to tell him when to stop, which he did when the glass was overflowing. They drank half the bottle, took a nap and then went to the launch. It lasted only an hour and a half but the drinks bill came to, Banville thinks, something like £4,000. Later, someone suggested to Christy that a better title for the book would be *Up All the Nights*, as he was celebrating so much. At the party, Banville chatted to one of Christy's brothers, who was drinking a pint glass of what looked suspiciously like brandy. After only an hour, everyone was 'falling down drunk'. The buzz around the book that night was phenomenal.

The next day, Banville went with Farrer to meet Christy. As he recalls, 'David took me out there . . . Christy was such a wreck. He was seriously, seriously handicapped and none of it was nice but he was very brave.' In retrospect, Banville feels the letter he wrote to Christy was somewhat patronising, as, he says, 'It's a good book; considering where it came from, it's a wonderful book – but not *great*.'

When the novel was finally reviewed in the press, the reaction from the critics was similar to Banville's initial response. The *Irish Times* wrote, '*Down All the Days* will surely stand beside Joyce and in front of all the others . . . has Dublin writ large and writ for all time.' The *Sunday Express* in London called the book 'A great novel. Unforgettable.' *Life* claimed the book was 'a joy to read'; *Cosmopolitan* magazine called it 'an instant classic'; and the *New York Times* said, 'Nothing quite like this book has been known in literature.'

When Bernard Share reviewed the book for the *Irish Times* on 9 May 1970 under the heading 'Father, Dear Father', he wrote:

> The stasis of situation is mirrored in the casting and shaping of the book. Nobody goes anywhere or does anything, at least not in the sense in which today's more mobile Dubliners would understand; nothing much happens above the bed and bread lines – no politics, little polemics, no strangers intrude into the tight circle of family and old acquaintance. There is a great deal of drinking, shouting and knocking about. Children proliferate like rabbits, die like alley cats in holes and gutters. The richness of the cursing – unquotable alas on

this side of the wall of gentility – points up by contrast the poverty of a social structure in which the horizon can be fixed no further than the Friday wage packet. The structure is hierarchical: Father, drunk or sober, knows best.

In all, Secker & Warburg had five offers from top paperback firms, thirteen Continental bids, including six from Germany, and bids from four film companies. Banville remembers Farrer telling him he had forty-eight offers from foreign publishers for the book. Aubrey Davies, one of the directors of Secker & Warburg, wrote to Christy telling him about the interest in various translation rights:

> Another hat I sometimes put on is selling foreign rights. The response to your book has been fantastic. Forty-nine requests from publishers in eleven countries from Japan to Helsinki, via Israel. I shall tell you the outcome country by country . . . while I was in Paris at the end of last week there were two notes about the book. It is all very funny – one paper translated the title as 'Down With All the Days' and, in their blissful Gallic innocence, not having set eyes on the book, said the book was very sad! However, 'Le Figaro' translated the title correctly. You have written a superb book and may I add my humble plaudits to the vast, well deserved mound.

Everyone at Secker & Warburg was excited. Farrer wrote to Christy telling him:

> The news continues to be excellent. We have agreed terms for a French edition with an advance payment of £7,500. The German edition isn't yet settled but there will certainly be one and the advance will be very large. There will also be a Swedish edition with an advance of £800 and a Dutch edition with an advance of £750. There will, I suspect, be more countries to follow . . . we originally printed 6,000 copies of Down All the Days but

> so big has been the advance demand that we yesterday
> ordered a reprint of a further 9,000 copies . . .

On one day in 1970, Secker & Warburg sold 1,500 copies of the book.

The letters that Christy wrote religiously peter out at this time; one imagines he was too busy and too excited to write to anyone. His dream was now a reality. He had been aching for years and years to get *Down All the Days* into print. The idea for the book had been in his mind for over a decade and he had said to Katriona Maguire that he had to get the book out of his system no matter what – he didn't care if it was successful or made lots of money but he *had* to write it.

The final version of the book shocked his family and friends. Instead of maintaining the charming innocence of *My Left Foot*, Christy created a raw and wild world in *Down All the Days*. Sex, death and physical abuse are all topics covered in vivid, almost painful detail in the text. What is more, in part of the semi-autobiographical novel, Christy employs a stream-of-consciousness writing technique. The narrator's voice jumps from a small boy observing the world of Dublin around him to voicing the thoughts, fears and opinions of his family or even strangers on the street. In some scenes, Christy has rats eating the father's head in dream-like, confused sequences; wet dreams are recounted in extreme detail and those same dreams include conversations with legless, half-animal women. Sex is everywhere in the book and so is drinking. Nothing in *Down All the Days* is sweet or charming; in fact, its power derives from its absolute insistence on being as honest a story as Christy could tell. In its detail, the novel has Dublin and the Browns' family life so intricately and perfectly described that the reader feels as if he or she grew up next to Christy, watching it all with him.

Chapter Sixteen, which Banville refers to in his letter as 'the loveliest piece of prose I've seen in a long time', is a short one, only four pages long. It deals with the emotional reaction of the central character (disabled like Christy, unnamed and known to the reader only as 'the boy') to puberty and with his fear about his father's abusive behaviour. It tells of his horror at seeing his sister shave off the beautiful 'soft dark sweat-limp hair' from under her arms. The playwright Frank McGuinness says that this section of the novel struck him particularly, as it did Banville, and that this image has stayed with him since he first read *Down All the Days*.

Perhaps most important is the rhythm and poetry of the passage in question. It is clear that someone who understood and deeply loved poetry wrote the prose. It is as though Christy is revelling in words, almost bathing himself in them, his inability to speak combined with his incredible capacity to learn equating to a writing style which is oceanic in its proportions. He uses adjectives prolifically and the rhythms of the sentences are influenced by his inability to speak. If one attempts to read the passages out loud, one finds that there is no room to breathe, no rest, so to speak. The reader is overwhelmed with words and finds herself almost drowning.

However, the prose is balanced by the precise details Christy loved to use, and so the audience is immersed in the story and the reader finds herself inside the text, much like a dream. When reading *Down All the Days*, rather than listening to a story being told, one is put almost uncomfortably inside it. The last section of the chapter that moved Banville so much and left such an impression on McGuinness reads:

> Once, when he had seen his father touch his mother's hair almost timidly, a throb of joy and absurd ecstatic hope filled him; the moment burnt bright and perfect, full of a wild sweetness as when sometimes he fervently lost himself in prayer, the moment dropping into his mind like a first spring blossom; then almost instantly it was gone, broken, washed away on the harsh returning wave of his father's voice demanding his supper. Nothing of peace or charm lasted longer than it took his beating heart to

feel it, and he was back once more in the walled garden of his thoughts, chasing the shadows of such moments, listening always rapt and intent for the wings of his ambiguous angel, the touch of felicitous fingers upon his brow that turned always and abruptly to a vicious cheek-stinging slap dashing the tears from his eyes.

Awkward as any animal, and more immensely mute, he was learning to grow and live without being blinded by the stars.

Stars were blinding Christy in 1970. The critical and commercial success of *Down All the Days* must have overwhelmed him. His family and friends, though, swear that he had little time for frivolity and that he did not become pompous on attaining the status of world-famous author. McGuinness notes that the book would probably have been banned if someone who was not disabled had written it. Christy, with the enormous obstacles he had faced in his life, seemed to become an exception to the literary moral rule of the time. He laughed several times with his family about the idea that the book might be censored; the thought of shocking people pleased him. Christy always liked to be provocative. As he wrote to Katriona on 26 March 1962, explaining why he was sending one of his plays to the BBC rather than to RTÉ:

> the stuff I *like* to write, wouldn't have 'an earthly' with the gaggle of stuffed geese who run the station and who decide what we as Irish are to be shown and what we are not to be shown. This is not to say that I concern myself only with 'outlawed' subjects such as sex relations, religion, violence, etc. – it is more true to say that I am merely experimenting with these things as potential art-forms and expressions of dramatic conflict, and I am not at all concerned with if it is 'right or wrong', for that is something which is intensely personal and quite unanswerable by any criteria of general judgement.

Christy was now seen as a major figure in the literary world of Dublin. The reception and reviews he received were awesome. Yet his disability was still at the forefront of many people's minds, as can be seen in *Life*'s take on his work:

> Hats off to Christy Brown . . . who has written a whole novel – and a superb one – with the little toe of his left foot. How he even manages to shift the key on his typewriter amazes me, but according to his publisher, Brown had laboriously pecked out *Down All the Days* in this fashion for a period of fourteen years . . . He makes his shattering disabilities function for him as a symbol of the Ireland he knows. Just as Yeats saw a symbol of Ireland in statuesque Cathleen ni Houlihan inspiring her men to valiant deeds, and the embittered, exiled Joyce saw his country as 'an old sow that devours her farrow', so Brown's vision is a society so spiritually crippled by hopelessness and recklessness, by whisky and poverty, that only a literal cripple can see it for what it is.
>
> Disinherited of everything else, and crippled in more ways than they can even realize, Brown's characters handle an alien language with such verse and innate poetry that they redeem both the language and themselves from the evil days into which both have fallen.

The next step was the book's publication in the USA. The famous American editor Sol Stein (who had worked with James Baldwin and Elia Kazan) first heard of Christy through David Farrer. Stein and his publishing partner Patricia Day would often meet Farrer in London on scouting trips, looking for books that might do well in the American market. They considered visiting Farrer to be both business and pleasure. Patricia Day read *Down All the Days* in typescript and she wanted to make an offer on it instantly. Stein was not so sure. After reading it, what he was certain of was that the book would need serious editing. He had written a dissertation on James Joyce and he saw in Christy's novel a great piece of Irish literature, rich with imagery, lyricism and social commentary. But he was not sure if the book would float financially. Day and Stein discussed the matter and she remained adamant that Christy's novel was something quite special. They then decided to place an offer on the American rights to the book. Originally, Stein suggested to Day that they should offer Farrer $500 for the rights but Day persuaded him to increase the sum to $2,000 – she felt less 'was an insult'.

Christy and Sol Stein first met in Kimmage in 1969. Farrer took Stein with him to meet Christy and discuss the American publication of the book and Stein being, in his own words, 'the brash American', decided to ask Christy if he could race him around the block in his wheelchair. Christy thought the idea was great and laughed as he told Stein he would love to have a go. They raced around the neighbourhood laughing like mad, and having good craic. Following that meeting in Kimmage, Stein decided to use Christy as a promotional tool. After he had procured the rights to *Down All the Days*, various PR people and others (including Farrer) had warned Stein that Christy was too provocative to be interviewed – after all, how would that work, anyway? Christy could barely be understood and he had a wild temper and a drinking problem. But Stein thought Christy would be fantastic at promoting his own work, so he ignored everyone's advice and Christy went to the USA to do a promotional tour.

The editor of the main newspaper in Michigan, the *Detroit News*, owed Stein a favour. He gave Christy's novel a front-page spread, and the book became a bestseller in the state. Stein then arranged for Christy to appear on the *Today* show, one of America's biggest breakfast programmes, watched by millions. Ordinarily, the programme did not film outside the studio because it was expensive but Stein called in yet another favour and a crew went out to the Moores' house in Stamford, where Christy and Seán were staying, to do the filming. It took over two hours to get six minutes of useable film. Christy was sweating profusely, and trying to get him to say something that could be clearly understood caused major problems for the journalists from *Today*. Stein was worried that the interview would not be aired. He called his contact at the programme and asked what was happening. 'The NBC executives watching it now are crying. I think it'll run,' was the answer he got.

Stein asked Christy what he would like to do now that he had made a major impact on American audiences and his book was doing well. 'I want to do a live interview,' Christy told him, 'like all the other authors do.' So Stein contacted more people and arranged a taping session with David Frost at Manhattan's Little Theatre.

According to Stein, Christy's appearance on *The David Frost Show* on 25 August 1970 in New York nearly didn't happen. Apparently, as soon as Frost saw Christy, he told the cast and crew that he was concerned about the feasibility of the interview. As a result, Christy sat in his wheelchair for quite some time in front of a live studio audience while that decision was being made. Stein was unsure of what he ought to do. He knew from having spent time with him that Christy could make certain noises – his 'p's and 'b's were quite clear when he pronounced them carefully and Seán would be there to interpret what Christy was able to say, if need be. He told the staff on the show to fetch Christy a small glass of water, with just a touch of whiskey in it. He explained his plan to Christy and Frost and the decision was made to proceed.

When Frost went on stage, he did a brief introduction and then turned to Christy and asked him what he would do now he had written such a successful book. Christy smiled and made a gargling noise in his throat and the audience laughed and applauded. Frost then asked what he wanted to do besides gargle his whiskey. Christy replied, 'Buy a pub,' and because of the enormous effort it took for him to speak these three words, the audience responded with thunderous applause. Frost asked Christy what he would do in the pub once he had bought it.

Christy simply smiled and began to sing 'When Irish Eyes Are Smiling'. Then Frost enquired whether Christy had any advice for the audience and the viewers. Christy smiled again and said, 'Love life.' At that, the studio audience rose to their feet, applauding and cheering. Until then, Frost had always refused to say which of his interviews was the best but after meeting Christy, he declared this to be his best ever and immediately invited him to appear on his programme in Britain.

Just as his career was taking a turn for the better, Christy's personal life was about to run into serious problems. Beth had guided Christy through the emotional pitfalls of writing the novel, a difficult process that was exacerbated by his alcoholism. Seán remembers, while staying in Connecticut one summer, coming into the Moore house very late one evening and hearing Roberta Flack's classic track 'The First Time Ever I Saw Your Face' echoing through the house. As he walked past the front room, he realised not only that he might well be interrupting a very private moment for the secret couple but also that his brother had found a woman who adored him and that they had fallen deeply in love. Beth had disciplined Christy to write *Down All the Days*, allowing him to drink only in the evenings after he had completed bouts of constant work during the day. It would be fair to say that without Beth Moore, Christy might never have produced *Down All the Days*. She read his first drafts before anyone else and, over many long hours of conversation, secret love letters written and poems exchanged over the Atlantic, she fell in love with the words he wrote and the mind that had created them. Now, her and Christy's private space – the book they shared and the work they did together – was being shown to the world, and doing very well. All the while, though, Beth remained in the background and she did not like it.

She had suggested on the evening of the Frost interview, before she drove Seán and Christy to the studio in Manhattan, that she, rather than Seán, interpret for him. Christy picked

Seán over her and she was very angry. On the way home, she cursed him and said that he was ungrateful and cruel and when they finally arrived back at the house, she was so incensed she took one of the paintings that he had given her out of the house, placed it under one of the car wheels and reversed over it.

Christy was not happy. A note from one of the editorial coordinators at Secker & Warburg evidences his irritability during this period. After seeing the new cover for *Down All the Days*, Christy wrote to them complaining about the image. As he was now a powerful and popular author, the reply was swift and very polite:

> . . . here is a copy of the new jacket, which I hope you like as much as I do. I guess I should apologise for using the photograph which you say makes you look like 'both Methuselah and the original Darby O'Gill', but quite honestly, Christy, I like this photograph very much.

Shortly after Beth's violent loss of temper, Seán and Christy decided to leave the Moores and went to stay on a lake in upstate New York with a hippie couple whom they had met during the summer. The tension in the Moore house was just too much for the both of them and they – particularly Christy – wanted to enjoy every minute of the success. Christy's leaving her home alienated Beth. Somehow, now that she was not required to take care of him, she could no longer keep hold of him and, although he told no one, he had decided that he would end their relationship. When he was interviewed by the local paper, the *Stamford Advocate*, on 22 July 1970, he did not mention staying with Beth nor her helping him with the writing of the book. Instead, he told them he wanted to go to the local pub. When asked what he would do there, he wrote as a reply: 'I will be meeting with friends and drinking and cursing; that's what pubs are for.' The journalist who penned the article wrote: 'Mr Brown, whose penchant for drinking is one of those truthful clichés like the twinkle in his eyes, doesn't like the way many reviewers have made a cliché of his success story, and prefers his writing to be judged on its merit.' When asked whether or not he liked America, Christy said he did very much but that he thought 'children here miss out on the simplicities'. When asked to elaborate, he said, 'It's hard to put your toes on it.'

Christy took advantage of his new-found financial freedom and bought himself a new wheelchair, which was just the beginning of his spending the large royalties he earned from the book. He nicknamed the wheelchair 'Olympus' (referring to the seat of the gods) and was amazed at the freedom it gave him. One afternoon, however, while he and Seán were sitting around with friends drinking and relaxing, he took his new chair outside for a spin. An hour later, Seán heard Christy screaming at the top of his lungs for someone to help him. His chair had got stuck in the tarmac path, which had melted in the intense American sunshine, and he had been trapped there for ages. True to Brown form, Seán just laughed and left him there, telling him he would be better off with his boxcar Henry.

If you ask any of the Browns whether or not Christy changed when he became famous, they all say the same thing: that he did not change in the least. He was, as he told everyone on the Frost show, a man who truly believed everyone should love life, and his money and fame were simply new territories to be explored with the same vigour with which he always approached living.

It was when Christy was at the height of his success that Noel Pearson first met him. In May 1970, Ulick O'Connor invited Pearson to the opening of an exhibition of Christy's paintings, held in the Agnew Somerville Gallery in Dublin. O'Connor remembers that during his speech, he said what a pity it was that Christy's mother, Bridget, was not there to see her son's remarkable achievement. Without hesitation, Christy butted in and shouted, 'She is here, she is here!' and O'Connor felt, for just a moment, that in a strange way she was.

Pearson and Christy spoke briefly when they met at the exhibition and they kept in touch. As Pearson remembers it, 'We used to hang out all the time. I became his agent – not that I did any business for him, he was amazingly independent. He would just turn up and there'd be a taxi man on your doorstep saying, "He's waiting on ya." We were in College Green at the time. He used to come down and see me and he used to drink like a fish!

'We went back to his house one night and I said I didn't believe that he typed up all the manuscripts himself. So he whipped off his shoe – he had an IBM 'Golf Ball' typewriter, which was on a little platform – and he typed away with his toes. The text was perfect – perfect! But the sweat started pumping out of him 'cause there were two sheets of carbon paper – he had to give two copies to the publisher – and he was trying to marry the carbon paper up with his toes. So I said, this is stupid, you know. How about using my copy machine?

'You had to listen to understand what he said. It got better as it went on. Your ear had to get in tune with what he was saying. I had to be at least twenty minutes with him. But he was great. I mean, he had amazing courage and he never thought there was anything wrong with him, in a way, even though, of course, he knew there was.'

Pearson is from the same area of Dublin as Christy and, like him, is from a family with thirteen children. Until 1970, however, he didn't know Christy or any of the Browns. He recalls that the family had a formidable reputation in Kimmage and so he kept well clear of them. He remembers, 'I didn't know him when I was a kid. He was in a boxcar then. You stayed away from them, like, they were tough. The old fella [Christy's father] was called "Squabbler Brown". He settled everything with a head-butt. So they were a really rough family. It was a tough time then but it wasn't violent, there were no knives or guns . . . My mother had thirteen, and she was eighty-six when she died. It was quite normal to have a large family then; like, a small family was eight or nine. The Catholic Church was very powerful.'

Pearson was managing the folk group The Dubliners in 1970 and had no idea that hearing Christy's story one evening would eventually take him to Hollywood. He was astounded by the audacity of this man who wrote with his foot and had a vibrant love for living that he found inspirational.

That same evening at the opening of the exhibition, Kevin McClory, an Irish screenwriter, producer and director, bought three of Christy's paintings. McClory had started his career at Shepperton Studios and had worked as an assistant director to John Huston on *The African Queen*, *Moulin Rouge* and *Moby Dick*. He is most famous for his later work as producer on the James Bond film *Thunderball*. But in 1970, he was convinced Christy's story was perfect for film and that night he announced that he was opening discussions with Christy to buy the film rights to *Down All the Days*. McClory became an avid fan of Christy's after meeting him at the exhibition and it was through him that Christy would meet the actor Richard Harris.

On 16 June 1970, McClory asked Christy to meet Harris and himself in Dublin city for a few drinks. After that, he would sometimes call at Stannaway Road just to drink and talk about literature and theatre with him. As Christy's sister Ann remembers it, when Harris dropped in to say hello, there was an awful lot of drinking and effing and blinding. When Harris went on the BBC chat show *Parkinson*, he read an enormous poem for Christy entitled 'Christy Brown Came to Town'. He told Parkinson about Christy:

> . . . and so with his left foot he taught himself to type and he typed a book called *Down All the Days*, which has become a kind of classic in English literature. Well, I had the opportunity of meeting Christy Brown and reading passages of his book on television. When I met him I wrote him this poem.

Harris was in awe of Christy; so much so, in fact, that he romanticised the story somewhat for the benefit of the studio audience, telling them and Michael Parkinson that Bridget had read Yeats and Shaw to Christy when he was a child. There was no way this was possible: those books were never in the Brown house until Dr Collis brought them to Stannaway Road. Harris went on to read his poem live on air. It talks of Christy 'making his face shine upon us and throwing from the seaweeds of his wisdom iodine to heal the wounds of a waiting world'. Later, after Christy's death, Harris's loyalty to him was such that he invited Seán and Ann to a one-man show he was doing in Dublin, where he announced he had a special song he wanted to do for them. He then sang the Hollies' 'He Ain't Heavy, He's My Brother'.

Chapter Eleven

A WEDDING

So the bold Sol Stein is no egghead. I'm always wary of intellectual publishers. They offer you patronage instead of hard cash and swear by high heaven to make you famous by the time you have spent your first decade in eternity. I'd like the fruits of my labour here and now, Mister, if it's all right by you, while me ole genes and hormones and chromosomes are still healthy and active enough to enjoy themselves. I bequeath my fame to posterity and good riddance to it. I never saw a corpse yet that could sit up and drink a pint of stout however famous he might have been and I like my creature comforts while I'm still a mortal creature. Give us this day our daily bread and I don't mean the kind you slap butter on. So here's to shrewd Sol Stein and his ilk, and may the hair on his chest increase and multiply as long as he looks after my temporal welfare and starts the money rolling in.

Being poor, or even semi-poor, is such a drag, it's positively degrading, and destructive to one of my extreme fastidious-ness and sensitivity. I was born to be rich and rebelasian and to wallow in mistresses and Napolean brandy . . . I was not born to spend my days on cabbage and potatoes and to perish of TB or pneumonia in a damp smelly peeling little dungeon in the concrete wilds of south-west Kimmage with not even a dog never mind a mistress to my name.

No bejasus I wasn't and if I don't have all I wish myself to have by my fourth decade I'll wrap up this mortal coil once and for all – if not by a bare bodkin then via the ole gas fire and a shilling in the meter. Once you get used to the idea dying is not bad, but it's so much more acceptable if you've lived a little beforehand. And there are so many lovely luscious women around just waiting to be . . . befriended?

I'm glad you're happy about my book, now that the great flood of euphoria has receded somewhat and I return once more to cold reality. I am scared as hell about it. As of now everyone is saying well done, how marvellous, bravo, how thrilling, what a clever bloke you are, and thumping me on the back 'til I'm black and blue. But will they want to know me when the book comes out and they read the bloody thing. They will probably call me Judas Iscariot and a lot less biblical names for painting such a lurid picture of their little cosmos, conveniently forgetting that it is my world and that I am in it too. Just as lurid and obnoxious and dirty-minded and animalian as any of the others in it. At the very least I'll bet there'll be a lot of red faces and forgettable silences upon the emergence of my little opus.

I dare say it's foolish and unmanly of me to worry about the possible repercussions now. I wish I could be brash and flamboyant and indifferent, but I'm not. I do care about what people think of me which is a great weakness and that's how it is. There you have me. It's nothing to do with an image, I don't know what the word means and anyway I doubt if I ever had one; at least I sincerely hope not. I am not very good at wearing masks, I just like to know what others think of me, as me. I mean I don't believe I am a complete fraud all of the time or totally unacceptable as a person. I am no great shakes as a writer or a painter . . .

I may be spending a fortnight in London over Christmas . . . the usual exotic places, but seeing you seems to be a lost cause, I just mention it in passing. I face the coming year of 1970, like a man facing the firing squad. Well, at least let's hope the bullets don't turn out to be blanks. Let me like a soldier fall. Whistle over the sea to me, dear.

Love, Chris.

Christy Brown, writing to Margaret Forster,
reprinted in the Sunday Times, *25 January 1970*

It was at a party in London in 1971 that Christy met his future wife, Mary Carr. As it was told in the film, Mary was a nurse who met Christy after he gave a reading of *My Left Foot* at a fund-raiser for cerebral-palsy patients. The last shot of the film is of Christy and Mary sharing a bottle of champagne and toasting Dublin; the caption afterwards tells the audience the date of their marriage. In typical Hollywood fashion, a happy ending was provided. However, the truth about their marriage is rather different. In real life, Mary was a lesbian, a prostitute and an alcoholic. She worked at one stage in a dentist's office, answering phones and dealing with patients, but she did not hold the job down for very long. Her drinking and abuse of other substances did not allow for her to have any kind of a serious career.

Asked about the girl his brother married, Seán Brown says, 'I know for a fact she was a prostitute. When I first met Mary in London in 1968 or 1969, she was the girlfriend of one of my good female friends, Mal. They were living as a couple and Mal was living off Mary. Mary made her money by sleeping with people. I know she abused prescription drugs and alcohol, although, as far as I know, she never used anything else. Christy loved her but it wasn't reciprocated, because she wasn't that kind of person. If she loved him like she said she did, she wouldn't have had affairs with both men and women.

'I think it was a bad move from the start, as far as Christy's own health and happiness were concerned. There were too many problems. Mary would never settle down in Dublin with Christy. She alienated him from his family by moving to Kerry and then to Somerset. She wanted him well away from his family. Christy's writing and his painting went downhill after a few years of marriage. I find it sad that Mary never showed any interest in his painting or writing. For years, I have felt a lot of guilt about Christy and Mary's marriage and I rue the day he ever met her. I feel she took advantage of him in more ways than one.'

She and Christy would stay together until his death in 1981 and there were those close to Christy who believed that her alcoholism and neglect contributed to his rapid decline, even that she was responsible for manslaughter.

When Christy first saw Mary at the party at Seán's house in Bayswater, she was only twenty-three years old. She would later tell journalists that she was not intimidated by him. Christy was sitting in the corner of Seán's flat drinking vodka through a straw when he and Mary caught one another's eye. He did not notice her at first but when he finally did, he kept glancing over at her. They ended up sitting next to each other on the couch in Seán's flat, which was crowded with people. They talked about James Joyce; she would say in several newspaper articles that she understood his speech easily at once. They spoke for a few hours and he learned she was Irish, from the south-western county of Kerry, but she had spent most of her life in England. Christy was desperate to see Mary again. Before she left, he asked her if he could write to her. She said yes. Two weeks later, he told Seán that he must pass on a letter from him to her.

Mary had been married before, as she told journalist and author Hunter Davies in an interview published in the *Observer Magazine* in 1989, when she was very young; she was divorced by the time she was twenty. Her first husband, whom she refused ever to name, was 'famous for fifteen minutes in the '60s'. When they divorced, she said, she got 'some money and a house in Greenwich'. When Christy discovered what she did for a living is uncertain but he would not have judged her (he was a true romantic and always wanted to see the best in Mary). It was not until the last year of his life that he would write to friends and family and tell the truth about the dire situation that their marriage created.

After their first meeting, Christy wrote letter after letter to her and a few months later, while on a trip to Kerry to see some of her relatives, she came to Kimmage to meet him. Mary stayed with Christy in the house that he was having built in

Rathcoole (four miles from Stannaway Road). It was purpose-built for him to accommodate his wheelchair. It had large spaces to allow easy movement, doors that could be easily opened and no stairs. Christy called the house 'Lisheen' (an Irish word meaning a small fairy fort, a place of magic). Ann and her family shared the new house with him. A breezeway separated the two parts of the house so that Christy would have his space to work and Ann had privacy with her husband, Willy, and their children. Christy was infatuated with Mary, more so than he had ever been with any other woman. He often referred to her in letters as Boticelli's Venus.

In the same year that he met Mary, Christy decided he must end his relationship with Beth. Over the years, Deac had become increasingly troubled by his wife's affair with Christy, which had not remained a secret. In the summer of 1970, he had suggested that they adapt to 'conventional wife-sharing'. Christy had rejected this idea at once but the situation just became worse. Deac had found their letters and had threatened to leave Beth and take the children with him. He became impotent and wrote letters to Christy explaining how Christy had caused him insurmountable problems in his marriage and his personal life. His inability to 'perform sexually, excessive drinking and need of a psychiatrist' were all a result, he believed, of the affair. In 1971, Deac and Beth came to London to help celebrate the amazing response *Down All the Days* was receiving from the media and its success. Christy met her in a hotel and told her he had found someone new and that he wanted to move on. Christy and Beth thought they would never speak again after they met in London. Although they did write to one another a few more times, they never again shared an intimate bond – either of love or friendship.

Christy was relieved to be rid of the complicated situation, which had torn him up for over a decade. On the same trip, he paid a visit to Mary and asked her to come to see him in Dublin. Presumably, he told her about ending his relationship with Beth as an indication of the seriousness of his dedication to their relationship; Mary would mention in the interview with Davies that Christy was 'a bit of a Romeo' and that he had been seeing a married woman for quite some time before she and he became a couple. She agreed to go to see him and a few weeks later, she arrived again in Rathcoole. For three days at Lisheen, they drank a lot and talked. On one of those nights, she told Davies, Christy called Mary into his bedroom and asked her if she would marry him. She was shocked and thought maybe he was too drunk to know what he was saying. Nevertheless, she said yes and saw him glow with happiness; but straight after agreeing to be his wife, she regretted it. He saw that she might not have meant it and so he just smiled and told her, 'Think about it.' Christy wrote to Seán, telling him:

> Let me just say that our relationship has deepened considerably since she stayed here as my guest at Easter, a fact which caused several raised eyebrows among family and friends which did not surprise me at all and which did not of course in the least affect my feelings for her. I would naturally respect your opinion if you have one to offer, again with the proviso that it could scarcely affect my own thoughts and emotions to any considerable degree . . .
>   God Bless,
>   Chris.

> P.S. I've fallen hopelessly in love with this beautiful blonde German Countess called Charlotte . . . but that's another story for another night.
>   P.P.S. I've started to write a play for the Abbey just tonight. It reads very well so far. I here and now invite you . . . to the first night – that's how confident I am that it will not only be accepted but acclaimed as a masterpiece . . . it says here.
>   P.P.P.S. Have you heard from Janet recently – you know, the girl in the flat downstairs from you? If you see

her, will you ask her did she get my letter, and if she did, why the fucking hell hasn't she answered it? I mean, I thought she was a lady . . .

Love, you bastard,

C.

Mary went back to London, and, as she said to Davies in 1989, she 'realised she missed him'. She discussed the idea of marrying Christy with her friends there, most of whom told her they thought it was a terrible plan. Others said maybe it could work but even they doubted if she would be able to give up her old lifestyle. Marrying Christy meant making a commitment, and not just a matrimonial one but a huge physical and mental one. He needed caring for all the time, as Bridget had done and now Ann did. If Mary got married to Christy, she would have to make sure he was fed and bathed and that his drinking did not spiral out of control. His disability combined with his personality and his addiction meant Mary would have to work at least twice as hard as most people do in a marriage. She thought about her options and decided what to do. Three weeks after he had proposed to her, she wrote to Christy and told him she wanted to marry him.

Meanwhile, Christy had decided to reward himself with a short holiday in the south of Ireland. He had been working hard dealing with what he referred to as 'the literary set', and he was tired of the 'non-stop parties'. The American journalist Bill O'Donnell met Christy on a Sunday afternoon in April 1971 at the Oyster Bar in Cork city centre. Christy looked exhausted. He had been touring for months to promote *Down All the Days* and Bill remembers thinking he looked 'spent and skeletal'. Roger Grant, a self-exiled, well-educated Irishman, introduced the two of them. On holiday in Cork, he had rung Bill in Boston and suggested he come to Ireland for a break. When Bill arrived, Roger told him he was with this writer, Christy Brown, and asked him if he would like to meet him. They drank in the bar all night. Bill had to take Christy to the toilet, as his drinking partners did, and after the Oyster Bar closed, they went out in Christy's car together, having decided to go back to Lisheen. Bill and Christy ended up 'on the juice' together for a week. Somewhere between Cork and Rathcoole they ran out of petrol. Christy found the escapade hilarious, as they had to go around old country lanes knocking on doors at two in the morning asking for help; he thought it was great craic. Eventually, they found a house with a petrol station attached; the man who owned the station cursed them but sold them enough petrol to drive back to Lisheen. When they arrived at the house, they decided to drink more. This time it was poitín, an Irish moonshine, illegal because of its high quantity of alcohol.

The next night, Bill read *My Left Foot* and as Christy watched him, he had an idea. He asked him to read the poem 'For My Mother', which he had written just after Bridget died. At first, Bill refused but Christy kept asking, so he relented and read it aloud. Christy listened and cried. In that week they spent together, Bill found Christy to be articulate and passionate about music, cinema and wine. He had, according to Bill, strong opinions on everything and Bill was always impressed by the scope of Christy's knowledge. He told the American that he had gone to Cork to escape his publisher, the public and his family.

After that week, Bill and Christy remained friends, exchanging airmail letters and phone calls across the sea; Bill visited Christy a few times in Ireland. He remembers his friend as irreverent and full of ironical views of life which made him 'laugh till my sides ached' and as a man who was caring enough to show Bill's six-year-old girl how she could type using only her left toe (he typed a poem for her as well). Bill was at Lisheen when Christy announced his engagement to Mary Carr. The Brown family were shocked, as was Katriona Maguire. Christy was very close to his brothers and sisters, and yet they had no idea that the romance had become so serious.

In July 1972, Mary went to live with Christy at Lisheen for three months before they were to be married. Christy asked Noel Pearson to organise the wedding and he told him he would be more than happy to do so. When Noel and Christy were working on the guest list together, Christy told Noel to 'invite the Duke of Edinburgh and the Queen'. Noel said, 'You're joking me!' and Christy said, 'Ah, give it a lash.' According to Noel, it didn't matter to Christy that he had never met them and was hardly likely to get them to turn up: 'He loved the publicity of it all.'

On 5 October 1972, at 1.30 p.m., Christy Brown and Mary Carr were married in a registry office on Kildare Street in Dublin. They had a luncheon reception on the coast, at the Sutton House Hotel in County Dublin. There was a head table for the bride and groom and several tables laid out for the guests. Gay Byrne sat with Patricia Sheehan and Kevin McClory; Ulick O'Connor, Richard Harris and all Christy's brothers and sisters who were then alive (Paddy, Mona, Ann, Seán, Eamonn, Francis and Jim) attended. Pearson says, 'The wedding day was phenomenal, it was a beautiful day. The sun was out, everyone was lying on the lawn outside Sutton House. I think it [Christy and Mary's marriage] lasted much longer than anyone thought it was going to last.'

However, the wedding was also a difficult affair, he recalls: 'It was all very tight, very tense, everybody was . . . thinking there was gonna be a row'. O'Connor remembers, 'He [Noel Pearson] organised the family generally. I remember Christy was in a chair and her ladyship was up front, not really behaving herself. I must say, I gave my congratulations to Christy but he complained bitterly about her already having gone off and had a lesbian affair in London and that sort of stuff – well, "bitterly" is the wrong word, he just said she'd done it, but obviously he was upset.'

There was some scepticism as to Mary's motivation for marrying Christy and his brothers, sisters and friends were somewhat suspicious of her, so the wedding could have been a disaster. Jim, the eldest surviving brother, was asked to make a speech to start the celebrations, in the place of Christy's father. Jim wouldn't give an ordinary speech from behind the table; he said he was 'no good at speechifying'. So he came out into the middle of the room and sang a song. It was 'Take Me Back to Idaho', which was the Browns' father's song. Pearson remembers feeling that it really broke the ice.

Christy had told Noel 'No whiskey' because he was worried that the drunker everyone was, the more likely it was that there would be arguments. He also told him, 'I don't want any Guinness.' He didn't want the wedding to be 'common'. The bar was kept open until four o'clock in the morning and when the reception champagne ran out, they drank pink champagne from the cellar. After the party, the couple went to the bridal suite and they were in such a state Seán had to help them up the stairs. He tried to get them to go to bed but they went out onto the balcony. Pearson went up to see them and he thought Christy 'was out of it. He didn't know where he was. And she was out of it, too . . . the straps were off her gown and everything . . . that was when the bar closed and everyone had to go.' Noel remembers that Christy and Mary then went back to Dublin, to a local pub in Kimmage, and that 'they were there till closing; they must have been in some state. I went home, 'cause I was thinking, this could end up a disaster. And they were giving out: "Where is that Noel? Where's the whiskey? He says he's been told not to give us whiskey. Who does he think he is?!"'

After the wedding, Christy and Mary left for the Caribbean; Kevin McClory had given the newlyweds two tickets and a paid hotel reservation as a gift. When they returned, they settled into Lisheen, while Christy began working on another novel and a new collection of poetry.

During this period, in the wake of the release of *Down All the Days*, Christy was at the height of his fame and the media were very interested in getting an interview with Christy Brown.

Hunter Davies (whose interviews with Christy and Mary are reprinted in his book *Hunting People*) was lucky enough to have a connection with him already. Davies' wife, the novelist Margaret Forster, and Christy had exchanged letters since 1965 and he had met Christy before all the hype about *Down All the Days* had started. For five years, Forster and Christy exchanged letters and he asked her several times if they might meet; she always said no. As Davies wrote in an interview with Christy printed in the *Sunday Times* in 1970, '[My wife] didn't want to [meet him]. She didn't want to disappoint him. She wanted it to go on for ever, all on paper.'

Forster did eventually meet Christy, as Davies remembers in the 1989 *Observer Magazine* article. Davies was interviewing him at his sister's house in London. Almost immediately, Christy begged Davies to take him to meet Forster and after much persuasion and a lot of drinks, he decided to bring Christy to see her. Davies thought his wife had heard them coming down the drive and that as they entered the house, she was hiding. He told Christy that she must be asleep; he responded by swearing at Davies and demanding whiskey. He was 'almost unconscious with the drink', according to Davies, but still he asked him to give his wife a shout in case she was there. He did and she 'came out of the room where she had been lurking'. She was 'horrified' when she saw the state Christy was in. They wrote only a few more letters to one another after their meeting. Forster burned almost all the letters he had sent her.

Christy corresponded with Davies too, but his surviving family remember that Christy came to resent him; he felt the man typified the journalist who would turn him into the ultimate stage Irishman as an easy angle that sold papers. Despite this, he agreed to another interview with him, again for the *Sunday Times*, in 1973, although at first he went out of his way to give sarcastic answers and be rude. Davies asked him, 'In what ways have you used money to overcome your handicaps?' Christy typed his reply:

My new-found wealth was really a problem at first, but then I hit on the idea of opening the first brothel strictly and exclusively for Christian Brothers. The girls have been carefully selected from the ranks of the Poor Clare's, a very charitable combination, don't you think? This area is very 'up and coming'. When I do eventually sell I'll make a handsome profit.

Hunter went on to ask him how he met Mary, and Christy replied:

Before I go any further, let me tell you how I feel about such questions. I cannot believe the general mental standard of the newspaper-reading populace has fallen so drastically that they can be regarded by and interested in the love life of a cripple trying to earn an honest living. I refuse to believe the average reader is as moronic as all that, unless we are breeding a new species whose minds are computerised and programmed exclusively to absorb the more inane outpourings of Miss Proops and others of her ilk, immutably bound to the agony columns of the daily and Sunday celluloids, at which prospect my very soul shudders. However, ours is not to reason why, ours is but to drink and sigh . . .

On 1 April 1990, after the success of the film version of *My Left Foot*, some of the material from Davies' interviews with Christy and one of the Irish writer's letters were published in the *Sunday Times*, under the headline 'Christy Brown on Christy Brown: in an unpublished letter, the author talks about James Joyce, suicide and beer'. This is just the type of media spin that Christy hated, although its being printed on April Fool's Day would probably have amused him.

Ann saw him become very angry once when she and her husband left him outside a shop on Grafton Street in Dublin city centre. He and his nephew Darren waited outside as she and her husband bought a few things. When they returned, they found Darren in tears and Christy swearing his head off. As the two had sat waiting, someone had come past and, out of pity, had dropped money into a cup that was attached to Christy's chair. Ann and her husband laughed, telling him he ought to stay on Grafton Street and get a few bob together so they could have some drinks that night, but Christy did not find it funny at all. Given this sort of occurrence, it is understandable that Christy Brown could be extremely sensitive when it came to dealing with the press. He hated to be pitied, and what he perceived as pseudo-intellectual journalists projecting their angles or sympathy onto him infuriated him, as did anyone trying to psychoanalyse him. It reminded him of the way he felt he had been treated by the DAA: as a disabled artist, not an artist with a disability.

Ann believes: 'He was angry, very angry. I think a lot of Christy's drinking had to do with his anger. He didn't say, "Why did this happen to me?" He was angry that he couldn't get up and go, he used to get angry because he was frustrated, watching all of us moving around. It was a brilliant mind trapped inside this body, you know what I mean? It was very, very hard for him.'

When Davies had asked him 'When did you last think of suicide?', Christy's reply was:

> I think you originally meant to put that question to either Harold Robbins or Spike Milligan. May I ask you a question instead: do you actually get paid for asking me all these immensely forgettable things? Hats off to democracy. Have a drink.

Christy was more reasonable in the answers he gave to another British journalist, Alan Brien, whose interview was published in the *New York Times* as an article entitled 'London: Christy Brown's triumph'. He was kinder to Brien, but not much. When asked what a typical day in his life was like, he answered:

What is a typical day in anyone's life? We do the things we have to do, which is not always the things we want to do. What is a typical night is a better way of putting it . . . I bang away at my long-suffering typewriter, or slash away at my easel. Trouble is I cannot sleep during the day! I should go to the theatre more, but somehow I always seem to change direction in transit and end up in the pub. Pity. I like the theatre . . . of course, I have a drinking problem . . . I can never get enough.

Any question which implied that he was any different to anyone else simply because of his cerebral palsy triggered a barrage of anger. Questions that were relevant to his work, such as what he liked to read, elicited less facetious answers:

I read as little as possible so as not to be corrupted by anyone else's literary maladies, having more than enough of my own. At the advanced age of seventeen, I encountered Dickens, and he has ruined my prose style ever since. I'm a very sensitive plant, I hate this ethnic thing about writing, it's an inverted form of snobbery . . . while I'd be the first to admit that many Irish writers have and continue to influence me, for better or worse . . . I don't regard myself as being a particularly 'Irish' writer. Maybe because I don't know exactly what that means.

Brien, like Davies, asked Christy if he often thought of suicide. As *Down All the Days* has no characters or incidents of suicide at all, Christy interpreted such questions as indications that journalists felt that since he was disabled, his life was not worth living. It is no wonder he often became angry. He told Brien, 'I'm not morbid or obsessed about suicide or dying. For, apart from my glaring inability to cope with it, I do enjoy living.'

In his article, Brien quoted Sol Stein as saying that Christy was 'the most lyrical writer he had come across since Dylan Thomas'. Brien felt the comparison was unhelpful and thought Christy closer to Behan, describing him as 'a fizzing, well-shaken bottle of sweet-sour stout that must overflow or burst'. This description again reflects the desire of the media to gawp at the ultimate entertaining Irishman. It is interesting that when Christy was likened to other writers, it was always to Irish authors. After he became famous, comparisons were constantly made between him and Behan. A more illuminating parallel might be with one of America's great writers, Thomas Wolfe, whom Christy adored. According to Noel Pearson, Christy's favourite book was Wolfe's novel *Look Homeward, Angel*, published in 1929. Wolfe's surreal prose style and use of biographical detail is much more like Christy's work than is that of many of the Irish writers to whom he is more often related. In *Look Homeward, Angel*, Wolfe's voice could almost be Christy's:

> He was in agony because he was poverty stricken in symbols: his mind was caught in a net because he had no words to work with. He had not even names for the objects around him: he probably defined himself by some jargon, reinforced by some mangling of speech that roared about him, to which he listened intently day after day, realising that his first escape must come through language . . .

Wolfe's narrator, Gant, is an alcoholic, a lost soul and a man whose dream is to carve angels for the world. Wolfe's book is about how none of us can ever go home again, how dreams are lost and can never be retrieved. If we do attempt to go back, all we find are empty pieces of memories, and those generally do not match what we believed to be the truth.

Although he clearly had his misgivings, in fact, Christy was enjoying the media circus enormously. When he appeared on *The Late Late Show* (Ireland's equivalent to America's *The Tonight Show* or Britain's *Parkinson*), he was in a similarly irreverent mood to that which he'd displayed during his recent print interviews. He drank in one of the local pubs in Kimmage for several hours before he went live on air. The popular host, Gay

Byrne, posed the question to Christy during the interview, 'What would you say to some who criticised your book harshly?'

'Fuck 'em,' Christy answered. Byrne was shocked and he said, 'I beg your pardon? What did you say?' Christy repeated his reply: 'Fuck 'em.' It is interesting to note that in Pan Collins' book entitled *It Started on The Late Late Show*, the author refers to Christy not as an author but as a 'medical subject', recounting that, on television, they 'always have a special appeal'.

Regarding the television appearance, Ann believes that: 'He didn't care, he never stopped, about what was right or what was wrong, I don't mean that in a bad way. But he would never stop to think of protocol, like, "Ah, well, I shouldn't say this or that." He thought, "Well, you either like me or you don't like me." But no, I have to say, he never regretted saying that.'

On 28 May 1973, Ulick O'Connor went to visit Christy and Mary at Lisheen. He had 'got to the stage where I could talk to him fairly well, despite his plundered speech'. He found Christy depressed and alone. Mary was away in London every second weekend. O'Connor's published diaries record that Christy told him, 'She's in London every month, pot and lesbian friends . . . she wants me to live in the country . . . I was lonely before I married her. But that was the loneliness of a writer. Now I feel a different sort of loneliness . . . if she leaves I will write an incredible poem. That's all I've left. To make art out of anguish. You have suffered, you are gentle. Mary wonders how you and I could be friends? She forgets we are Dubliners.'

O'Connor noticed that the toes with which Christy typed were covered in blisters. He visited Lisheen four or five times while Christy and Mary were there and each time he noticed that Christy did not look well.

In late June 1973, Christy had finished his second novel, *A Shadow on Summer*. Its plot was a thinly veiled account of the author's relationship with Beth Moore and his experiences in America. The blurb reads:

Riley McCombe comes to America, pitchforked from total obscurity in Dublin into fame as the brilliant author of a major bestseller. Staying in Connecticut with Don and Laurie Emerson, Riley finds himself becoming more and more involved with Laurie, who appoints herself his mentor as he struggles to write a new novel. But when he meets Abbie, a young and beautiful photographer who also feels she has something to offer him, Riley is not only torn between himself and his work, but also between the two women.

He told Seán in a letter of that June that he had sent the book on to David Farrer and he was 'quietly confident of his response'. After finishing it, he wrote to tell Seán that he and Mary were going to Kerry together to have a rest; he would leave off writing for a while. What was most unlike Christy was that he locked up Lisheen, 'just in case the boys from Kimmage decide to honour us with a visit, as they might well do, strictly in our absence, so our gaff will be strictly out of bounds for that reason'. He told Seán in the same letter that he wished he could send him a copy of his just released book of poetry, *Background Music*, but that he and Mary only had one. He once wrote in a letter to Patricia Sheehan how he felt married life could turn someone one knew well into a virtual stranger. This was how many of Christy's friends and family were starting to feel about him.

Background Music, Christy's second collection of poetry, was put out by Secker & Warburg and dedicated to Mary. The Irish writer Brendan Kennelly reviewed the work in the *Sunday Independent*, calling Christy 'a writer whose primary concern is emotional honesty'. Kennelly believed the collection had faults but that overall it was successful. Its problems were 'outweighed by its virtues of humane concern, compassionate awareness and essentially constructive, loving attitude towards life'.

While vacationing in County Kerry, Christy and Mary bought a cottage and decided to leave Dublin permanently. In the last months of 1974, they put Lisheen on the market and by April

1975 they had moved to a cottage on the Kerry coast. Mab Cottage (named for the initials of Mary Alicia Brown) was perched on top of the cliffs on Kerry Head; its back garden was a sheer drop of three hundred feet straight down to the crashing waves of the Atlantic.

Pearson remembers this as a chaotic period in Christy's life: 'His big threat was to put his foot through a glass window. He was always threatening suicide. There was a time when he was in one hospital and his wife was in another hospital and the two of them were in drying out. I'd known him all that time and then we kind of drifted.' After the move to Kerry, Christy began to use excuses for not seeing his family and friends, excuses they found bland and unbelievable.

Christy told Katriona in one of his letters:

> Alas and alack, I'm afraid going to Cork or indeed anywhere for that matter is out of the question for us right now and will be for months to come, as the builders have finally moved in and we want to be right on the spot all the time to ensure there's no hanging the latch this time around.

To Seán, he wrote:

> We were in Bristol last month on business, and saw a bit of the West Country – it's just beautiful. We just hadn't the time to make it down to London unfortunately – we had to get home as soon as possible on account of the dogs.

And to Sheehan:

> We almost certainly won't be able to make it up for your little soiree on Oct. 8th, but we'll be with you in spirit . . . it isn't easy for us to get up to Dublin very often . . . so sadly we must decline your invitation and miss the party.

None of Christy's close friends or family saw him more than once or twice in the last few years of his life. Ulick O'Connor would later write in his diaries:

> It seemed ludicrous to have relocated four years ago as he did to Kerry when he and his wife Mary bought a house. Christy's roots were in Dublin and he needed the oxygen of his family life and his own people around him to enable him to breathe. Kerry would have seemed like Alaska to him . . . Even moving to Rathcoole, Co Dublin . . . was I thought a bit far from his rearing . . . after he married Mary . . . things gradually went downhill. It was a daring experiment which didn't work. Mary was so often away in London, leaving him lonely as only someone locked up in a twisted body can be.

When Dr Robert Collis died in 1975, Katriona not only asked Christy to come to the funeral, she suggested he write something in memory of him. Christy replied:

> It was good to hear from you after so long, even though the occasion that motivated you was so sad. I still haven't altogether gotten over shock of Bob Collis' sudden death. In fact, it affected me to such an extent that I became physically quite ill and was unable to make the long journey up to the funeral . . . As to your suggestion that I should write some appreciation for him, no, dear Katriona, I think not, for I was too close to the man and whatever I might say would be bound to be misconstrued, for I would of necessity have to speak of his faults as well as his virtues, and in Ireland that kind of candour has never been understood or accepted. I agree with you that all the tributes that have appeared in print have rung hollow and I have a picture in my mind of people trying desperately to dredge up amusing anecdotes from the past that would pinpoint or highlight some of Bob's sterling qualities, a bit like gathering only the shiniest pebbles along an endless stretch of beach

in order to erect a tiny little mound of in memoriam. I think it is best to keep one's most precious monuments of remembrance within one's own heart and mind, away from the public gaze, for in that way you can tend to it and renew it all the more readily and sweetly from a much deeper well of affection.

From 1975 to 1976, Christy worked on another novel, *Wild Grow the Lilies*. The book relates the experiences of Luke Sheridan, a 'hard-drinking journalist' who passes his time at 'Madame Lala's house of pleasure'. His love interests in the book are Rosie, a 'sharp-tongued' prostitute, and Madame Lala's most alluring girl, 'Babysoft, whose work is her never-ending pleasure'. *Wild Grow the Lilies* runs into a farcical plot in which Sheridan follows a tip for a story about a murdered countess in the village of Howth on the outskirts of Dublin. The language of the book is tedious and overwritten and the storyline is all over the place. Christy was not drinking and working any more; he was simply drinking. From that time, only his poetry has any literary value. In Dublin, Ann read the book and knew something was wrong. Christy wrote that he 'continued to perspire poetry as if he was suffering from some glandular disease'. When *Wild Grow the Lilies* was published in 1976, it was a complete flop. Christy would never complete another novel or play.

Chapter Twelve

A FUNERAL

For about the past three or four years now it has got worse, my mental and physical condition has drastically deteriorated to the point where I have almost become a vegetable, unable or unwilling to think or feel intensely about anything and with logic long since gone out the window, if it was ever there . . . there have been moments of lucidity and fierce resolve, but they have inevitably evaporated like droplets of dew on hot mornings and the pattern of living from one bottle to the next reasserts itself with inexorable regularity.

. . . I've been in and out of psychiatric wards on at least half a dozen occasions, plus visits at home by doctors and what are laughingly described as social workers with amusing pretensions of psychiatric experience – usually callow, bearded young men who talk and smoke a great deal and ask you how your bowels are working . . .

The period of my incarceration in these hospitals varies: the 'drying out' process supposedly lasts for about ten days, with doses of anti-booze pills and in between regular meals; I think my longest stay was about a month, during which I became insufferably bored and just about able to function as a human being except on the most banal levels. Another disgusting symptom; I have become incontinent at both ends of the physiological scale both at home and in the hospital, which of course only tends to increase and heighten my self-loathing and renders thoughts of suicide both perfectly respectable and desirable . . . I'm just not

the man I used to be, I've only dim recollections of that
individual, like an old friend I used to know and with whom
I've lost contact . . . to quote John Clare – a memory lost.

Christy Brown, writing to Bill O'Donnell,
26 August 1981,
two weeks before his death

At the back of Mab Cottage, a large room surrounded by
glass gave Christy a place to think and write but his writing
had not been going well. The letters he wrote in the first few
years in Kerry say that he and Mary loved their home; but he
was a stubborn person and not the type to tell anyone that his
romantic dream was not turning out to be exactly what he had
hoped for. His later letters, such as the one above, suggest a
man bereft of hope and inspiration.

It was during this period of decline, in June 1978, that
screenwriter, novelist and film director Peter Sheridan first met
Christy Brown. Peter had seen Christy's infamous *Late Late
Show* performance with Gay Byrne in 1970, and, as a young
writer, he had been amazed by *Down All the Days*. He had
read it several years after its initial publication and was struck
by how much he could relate to in the novel. It seemed to
him that he and Christy had an enormous amount in common.
Here was a book that Sheridan felt would make an excellent
stage play. He wrote to Christy to say that he wanted to adapt
Down All the Days for the theatre.

Peter and his brother Jim had grown up in inner-city Dublin,
around the North Wall area. Peter discovered theatre in the
mid-'60s and became addicted. He and Jim avidly read the
works of Sean O'Casey, Brendan Behan, James Plunkett and
Christy Brown, all people who had placed working-class
Dublin on the page or the stage.

As Peter says, 'I grew up in the inner city, you know, Sheriff
Street area, North Wall area – a classic inner-city-Dublin kind
of upbringing. We were sort of lower-middle-class people in

a very working-class area, so from the time I discovered the theatre in the mid-'60s, I just had this huge, growing interest in all things literary, you know, and I discovered O'Casey, Behan, Plunkett, Christy Brown, all these writers who were writing Dublin or working-class kind of material. When I met Christy first, it was like that book [*My Left Foot*] gave him shivers, you know, 'cause he just felt it was a kids' book. He thought that it was this childish attempt at writing but it was actually a very good book. We writers often think that about our early stuff: that it's naive and childish and immature. It's actually that very quality that can make something beautiful. But he didn't like *My Left Foot* at all.'

Throughout the 1970s, the Sheridan brothers had been running the Project Arts Centre in Dublin. Peter describes them as 'the young kids on the block. We had youthful energy – we were as much into punk rock as into theatre.' He repeatedly told Jim that *Down All the Days* was fantastic and could easily be adapted and that they should try and do it. Christy was equally keen, so Peter was invited to stay with Mary and Christy in Kerry. When he and Christy discussed Christy's writing, the author expressed an enormous distaste for *My Left Foot*. He called it his immature juvenilia, decrying it as the bleating of a naive cripple. However, as Sheridan remarks, it is that quality of simplicity that makes the book 'very readable'. Still, Peter and Jim were keen to work on *Down All the Days* rather than on the memoir. The intense dramatic conflict of an intelligent individual encased in a wall of silence would, they thought, make for an excellent play.

Peter Sheridan was, at the time, an active alcoholic and he and Christy enjoyed the same tastes: pints of Guinness followed by whiskey shorts, in copious quantities. Shortly after Peter's arrival at Mab Cottage and following a discussion on the book and how an adaptation could best be created, the two men descended on one of the local pubs for a long session. At the time, Christy had been off the drink for several weeks, possibly even months, but Sheridan was a serious drinker. He had struggled with alcohol for years and years; in the late '70s, he says, he was 'in the throes of it'. He knew from Christy's work, and his television appearance, that his host had a serious problem with alcohol but he didn't know quite what to expect. According to Peter, 'I swear I'll never forget that night so long as I live.'

At the pub, Peter bought the first round, placing a pint of Guinness in front of Christy. He gaped as Christy drank it in one go, through a straw. It disappeared in seconds and then he wanted another. Straight after he'd finished the second pint, he wanted a third. Peter was amazed. After three or four rounds, he got a kick in the leg. 'Toilet,' Christy told him. Peter discovered that he had to take Christy to the Gents, undo his trousers, take out his penis and help him urinate. This was something Christy was quite accustomed to, but not Peter. He remembers thinking, 'I am holding Christy fucking Brown in my arms here, one of my heroes. He is pissing into a urinal and I am holding him and I could let him fucking fall 'cause I'm half drunk and this is mad.'

When they returned stocious drunk to the cottage, the two men discovered another shared passion: rock and roll. So they threw Jerry Lee Lewis's 'Great Balls of Fire' on the record player in Mab Cottage and danced together, 'drunk as skunks'. Christy was waving his left foot in the air and Peter danced all around the front room while Mary watched them both and laughed.

At one point in his stay, Peter tried to open a door for his host but Christy's left foot shot out to turn the knob and he told Peter, 'Don't open doors for me.' Christy had the entire cottage organised so that he could move around himself and Peter felt tremendous admiration for someone who so ferociously guarded his independence. He recalls Christy's penetrative blue eyes as 'the saddest eyes in the world', although, he points out, 'It wasn't all sadness.'

Peter went only once more to Mab Cottage, in 1979, and afterwards he and Christy worked on the play by correspondence. Eventually, on 30 April 1981, the play opened in the Oscar Theatre in Dublin. Peter and his colleague Chris O'Neill raised most of the finances for the production, with the help of the Arts Council. The Abbey Theatre, which had originally wanted the play, lost interest and would no longer back the project. Unfortunately for the play and its cast, the Irish hunger striker Bobby Sands died on 5 May 1981 and the British Embassy was not far from the Oscar Theatre. Riots ensued and a new piece of theatre was the last thing on anyone's mind. Very few people came to see *Down All the Days*; it closed two and a half weeks after its opening. When the play was reviewed in the *Sunday Independent* by Gus Smith, he wrote:

> Eleven years ago Christy Brown's autobiographical novel, 'Down All the Days', was ecstatically received by the literary giants. They hailed it in the tradition of 'Ulysses' – a distillation of Dublin, its raging men and lusty women. Extravagant praise perhaps, but for all that the work is a vital look at Dublin life in the deprived forties and also of course a study of Christy Brown's growing up.
>
> On Thursday night in the Oscar Theatre, the book, adapted by Peter Sheridan, arrived on the stage. If nothing else, there was a sense of occasion in the theatre, reminiscent of a Brendan Behan first night; an evident expectation among the packed audience . . . lovers of the drama of Christy Brown – and that is pure racy Dublin – cannot afford to miss this brave piece.

Peter and Jim had worked on the play for three years but the brothers were not dismayed by this relative disappointment. Jim told Peter, 'There's a fucking story in there and I'm gonna do it.' Ten years later, he would co-write and direct the film *My Left Foot*. When asked about his only meeting with Christy Brown, Jim says, 'He came in the theatre and we asked him what he thought of the play and it took him a minute or two to say that it was like *The Picture of Dorian Gray*. It took him so long to say it . . . you kind of had to relax to learn to listen to him, you know, it was unsettling in that way. And he had the fiercest eyes I'd ever seen – expressive, focused eyes. His head kept moving but his eyes were totally still.'

Perhaps another problem with the play, besides the riots which were going on outside, was Christy's insistence that the boy in the play (the character based on himself) should not speak. Peter Sheridan had done a lot of theatre work at the time and knew this simply would not work. No one can have a figure on stage who relays nothing through any form of language; even grunting or moaning were not allowed, in accordance with Christy's strict instructions. In the book, the main character rarely speaks. Rather, his experiences and emotions are expressed by means of a third-person narrative, and the reader hears his thoughts as though inside the boy's mind. In a dramatic adaptation, Peter and Jim needed the boy to engage with the actors on stage. In Christy's notes to Peter, he has written and underlined: 'Cripple boy should on no account speak. This is crucial. The narrator speaks for him, articulating his thoughts and emotions as well as telling the story.' Peter Sheridan felt this was nonsensical and that a silent figure who seemingly had no purpose on the stage would not work. Moreover, it removed the tension which he and Jim had so admired: the enforced silence which the central character had to endure.

Jim and Peter noticed in rehearsals how much the boy's silence was muting the drama. Peter attempted to explain the problem to Christy several times, but he would not relent. Certainly, when Jim came to make the film of *My Left Foot* seven years later, the young boy's struggle to be understood by those around him was central to its spellbinding quality. It is strange that only a few months before his death, Christy was unable to see how compelling this battle for self-expression could be for his audience. As Peter says, 'When you met Christy, you adjusted to his sounds and you adjusted to what he was saying. Although you would find it extremely difficult, it was part of the engagement . . . you were having to make these allowances and you would be trying hard to understand this person. You know what's inside his head is magical but he's finding it hard to articulate it. So he couldn't say big words, he couldn't express himself the way that he wrote and when he wrote, it was like he was articulating the inside of his brain and when he spoke, it was like another person. Now that's a very interesting conflict dramatically. And it's a torture as well.' Yet Christy wanted to take that away, believing, as Peter says, 'it [having the main character of the boy grunting] would make him look silly'.

Christy died only a few months after watching his life played out on stage. At the premiere of the play, Christy and Mary arrived half an hour late and refused to speak to Christy's former speech therapist Patricia Sheehan or his old friend Katriona Maguire. It was as though he did not like what he had become, and by seeing his old friends, he would be reminded of the person he used to be. The letters written in the last six months of his life tell of his constant attempts to dry out and to write, and of his ultimate dissatisfaction with his work. Christy had removed himself slowly from the working-class world of Dublin, but Dublin had been his lifeline. The city and its people fed his wicked sense of humour and his desire to be with people and have fun. By the time he arrived in Kerry, his writing was drying up. He had lost touch with many members of his family and his old friend Noel Pearson.

After living in Kerry for five years, in 1980 he and Mary moved to England. Mary and he had been fighting and drinking too much, and she felt a change would be good for them. She decided they should go to the village of Parbrook in Somerset, to a tiny cottage, with small rooms and a slight staircase, which he could not go up. Mary slept upstairs while Christy had to stay downstairs. According to some of his friends and family, she wanted Christy as distant from the Browns as possible. His anchor – his siblings – was too far away from him.

Even his personal writing changed at this time. The fire and ferocity of the wit and humour found in his earlier letters turned into stale niceties. He was exhausted and displaced, left in an intellectual and social no-man's-land. Yet again, no one could understand him, just as they hadn't in his earliest days in Kimmage. A shadow of his former self, Christy had no one with whom he could reflect, laugh or remember his earlier life. No one in the local pub would have known how to handle Christy's temper. No one would have understood his humour. No one would have known that he needed help when going to the lavatory. He was alone except for Mary and, by all accounts, she was not as able to help him as she should have been.

On 15 February 1981, seven months before he died, Christy went missing. None of his friends or family in Dublin could locate him. In fact, his 'disappearance' was the result of the move to England – he had not informed anyone close to him of the change. Dr Sheehan was so desperate to get in touch with Christy, she used all the contacts she had in the medical field in Ireland to try to find out where he was. She received the following reply:

> Dear Patsy,
>
> I spoke to Jack O'Connor the RMS of St Finian's Hospital this morning.
> Christy Brown was a patient in the hospital recently, but was taken out by his wife six weeks ago. They have no idea where he is now. I imagine the wife is hiding him somewhere. Good luck with your hunt for him.

Anyone who remembers Christy from Dublin or Kerry, in pubs or together with his friends and family, knew him as a

Rabelaisian hell-raiser. His poetry included lines such as 'no point crying over spilt sperm' and 'a glass of fine brandy renders some solace / and even at today's price / is cheaper than a full confession'. As Noel Pearson remembers: 'He was barred from a few of the pubs in Kimmage – you know, for kicking people with his left foot.' Christy's irreverent attitude, understanding of the futility of life, his distaste for the sacrosanct position the Catholic Church held in Ireland and the power it wielded in that era, and his hatred for mawkish sympathy – these were all genuine.

Morosely, prophetically, or perhaps both, his last collection of poetry, *Of Snails and Skylarks* (1977), contains many poems that broach death as a new and serious subject for him. Christy had written poems for friends who had died and he had dealt with death in his earlier books of poetry, but his final collection includes six poems meditating on his own mortality. In one of his last poems, 'Terminal Thoughts', he wrote:

> Death is so often a distinct non-event.
> Even the most incandescent of our lives
> can be ruined by a wretched curtain
> falling halfway between a belch and a sigh.
> And princes too once bluff and portly as Hal
> of far-famed bestialities and resplendent lusts
> seldom thunder top heavy into laughing graves
> but choke to death of obese surfeit on a mouldy wine
> cork
> and slide into ponderous boxes wormy with weariness.

On 6 September 1981, Christy and Mary shared dinner in their small cottage in Somerset. After drinking a bottle of red wine and some brandy and taking several painkillers, Christy ate his dinner of lamb chops and potatoes. He had to be fed with great care and watched closely as he swallowed his food. Sometimes food would get stuck in his throat and would have to be massaged down to prevent him from choking. On this occasion, this did not happen for some reason and he choked to death. He was forty-nine years old. After the inquest, the coroner announced a verdict of death by misadventure.

Only three months before, Christy had choked while Mary was feeding him. Ann was furious. She had lived with and cared for Christy for four years in the home they had shared in Rathcoole and she knew how easily food could get trapped in his throat if he was not watched carefully. Mary would later claim that she had turned her back for only a few minutes while she was feeding Christy, but Ann would contend that this was exactly how he could die so quickly.

The letters Christy wrote to family and friends in the months before his death, as well as interviews with various writers and artists who knew Mary well, suggest that she herself had a serious drinking problem. Numerous interviews mention her proclivity for taking off for long weekends, which she would spend with lovers (mostly female). Christy would be left to call for his driver to accompany him out and stay with him and care for him, or to ask friends to stay with him. During Mary and Christy's last months in County Kerry, the local doctor in Ballyheigue phoned Ann in Dublin to tell her that he had seen Christy and that he was 'in a very bad way'. He said not only that the couple's drinking had been out of control for some time but also that Christy was often covered in bruises and he believed Mary had inflicted them. But Christy had made his choice and told only a few friends and fellow artists how he missed Dublin and was saddened by Mary's behaviour. Yet he never left her and we have to assume that he never wanted to. It seems, though, that the relationship slowly eroded his soul, destroying his art and then him.

His novel *A Promising Career*, on which he was working at the time of his death, was eventually published by Secker & Warburg posthumously in 1982. It did not do well commercially or critically. The writer and critic Gillman

Noonan wrote in his review of the book for the *Evening Herald*:

> Sad indeed that the old left foot is no longer tapping and, as Beckett wrote of Behan, 'sorrow that no more.'
>
> In its time it tapped out a measure or two of human joy and suffering that left many a high-stepping buck of a scribbler standing and wondering how it had got there before him. It tapped best in the world it knew, the gutsy, bitter, hopeless, triumphant world of Dublin's working people.
>
> The language it used to describe them had a fine rough fibre that often shocked like a smack from an old rope that had seen many a world and was still around reeking of life.
>
> Beckett again, that vibrant priest of the impotent, wasn't it he who exclaimed on reading Christy's first book, 'What vitality!'
>
> That foot, however, when it strayed out of its world, lured perhaps by what the mind should think or the soul feel rather than by what the eye saw and the heart really felt, could end up in some quare old corners.
>
> *A Promising Career*, now sadly a posthumous novel, as the title might suggest, doesn't really end up anywhere, it passes rather through a world as would a weak yet quite stylish magnet through a cloud of sharp, dead filings, attracting a few and enlarging upon them as the only things around to look at.

Christy Brown fulfilled in his life his greatest wishes: to fall in love, marry and become a successful writer. According to his *New York Times* obituary, he had earned $370,000 just from his writing career. He had bought the Brown family home in Kimmage, had provided for his mother after his father's death, and indeed before that had given his whole family large sums of money. He had written a novel that had transgressed boundaries and cultural taboos and had pointed out the hypocrisies of the Irish culture in its attitude towards religion, sex and tradition. Christy achieved all that simply by doing what he loved to do. In his writing, he became an inspiration not just for disabled people but for anyone who feels unable to achieve whatever they set out to do. 'Dying,' he wrote in his poem 'End', 'is a curious thing.'

> I could die today with a little effort
> with a well-sprung wish I could die today
> quietly laughing or crying
> without trumpets
> without ceremony
> without drawing conclusions . . .

In another poem on death, he wrote:

> Come softly to my wake
> and drink and break
> the rugged crust
> of friendly bread
> and weep not for me dead
> but lying stupidly there
> upon the womanless bed
> with a sexless stare
> and no thought in my head.

If there was any tragedy for Christy, it was not to have thoughts in his head burning fierce and wild and waiting to be written. It seems that in the last months of his life, Christy had left himself behind. He called himself, in a letter to Bill O'Donnell, 'a bedevilled soul who knows the insides of hell quite intimately'.

Pearson remembers, 'They [RTÉ] called me in the middle of the night, at five o'clock in the morning, to tell me he was dead. They didn't tell me it was live on Irish radio. When he died he was skin and bone, he couldn't eat; he didn't eat.'

Christy's birth was a drama, as was his marriage, and his

funeral was no less so. His body was flown to Ireland, to Paddy Massey's funeral parlour on Thomas Street, Dublin, on 10 September 1981. The funeral and burial took place the next day. Christy was buried in Glasnevin Cemetery, laid to rest with his mother and father. Glasnevin is the unofficial national cemetery of Ireland and one of the oldest burial grounds in the city. Some of the most famous members of Irish society are buried there. Christy was interred in the same graveyard as Daniel O'Connell, James Clarence Mangan, Michael Collins, Kevin Barry, Maud Gonne, Alfred Chester Beatty, Éamon de Valera and Brendan Behan. His body was given a police escort from the funeral parlour in Dublin and all the close members of his family were also escorted from their homes to the viewing of the body and then on to the cemetery.

The day of the burial was somewhat unlucky; not only did the rain pour down in sheets but the gravediggers were on strike and Mary was over two hours late to the funeral because she was travelling from Kerry and her train was delayed. Everyone sat in the pubs around the cemetery waiting for her arrival. When the gravediggers found out that it was the author Christy Brown who was to be buried, they suspended their strike, picked up their shovels and marched to his plot, while whistling the theme from *Snow White*: 'Hi ho, hi ho, it's off to work we go.' As Christy's friend the Boston journalist Bill O'Donnell left Glasnevin, he overheard a latecomer mourner ask for Christy. 'You just missed him,' a man replied.

When Katriona Maguire, Christy's old friend and mentor, heard of his death, she was in Lourdes, working as a volunteer. It was a fitting place, as more than three decades earlier it had been Katriona who, through the Marrowbone Lane Fund, had organised Christy's first trip on his own, the pilgrimage to Lourdes. A very close friend of hers (who was also a social worker and a regular volunteer at Lourdes) brought with her one of the Dublin newspapers announcing Christy's death.

Katriona could not leave her work in France but she went to the Basilica to mourn the loss of what she calls 'one of the most amazing and interesting people I had ever known'.

Christy Brown's obituary in the London *Times* was printed on 8 September 1981. The last paragraph reads:

> The extraordinary thing about this remarkable human being was the first impression he made on people was of a particularly cheerful and gregarious man. Few can have met him without finding the experience life enhancing, and it is for his sense of fun, the obvious happiness of his marriage, his generosity, rather than for his physical handicaps, that his friends will remember him.

Jim Sheridan wrote an appreciation of Christy for the *Irish Times*. In it, he described the writer as having 'that Dublin defiance which refused to accommodate the slight mistakes of a maker'. Jim deemed *Down All the Days* 'one of the top five novels outside Joyce ever written by an Irishman', and he recalled meeting Christy while directing *Down All the Days* in the theatre:

> He was brought to see a preview of his famous novel. The immediate impression was one of courage. Not the kind of courage you associate with those who, less well off, manage to overcome life's vicissitudes, but that aura that surrounds those who have looked at all the fight life has to give them and you know they are going to be there in the fifteenth round.

In the *Irish Independent,* writer Brendan Kennelly also felt compelled to remember Christy. He wrote an article about Christy's work in which he said that it was his 'poetic gift of insight and language [that] made his novels special'. Kennelly pointed out that, above all, 'Christy Brown was an honest writer, with a deep-seated lyrical gift, psychological insight and unfailing humour that places him in the line of Beckett,

O'Casey, Joyce and Behan.' Christy Brown would have treasured this comparison. He had always said to his friends and family that what he most wanted was to be remembered as a poet. In his remembrance of Christy, Peter Sheridan wrote in the *Irish Times*:

> In the trauma of death your perception cleared and even the shadows burned balefully. You saw your father as he really was – the victim of his own circumstances. And out of the emotional turmoil experience you created your masterpiece and we cried with you for all the unnamable things, unnamably lost, down all the speechless years. Oh, you were so much more than an echo in a shell. And yes, the stars are near.
>
> From your immobile half acre you perceived life faithfully. And accurately. But more than that, you lived it. You were consumed by it. You cursed an indolent jockey as vehemently as a lack-lustre display by United (remember the '79 Cup Final) or the failure of the Dubs to overcome the Kingdom (for which you paid dearly to the natives of Ballyheigue). You loved Little Richard and Jerry Lee Lewis as passionately as the Dublin street balladeer, and we danced to them all. You were uncontainable, Christy.

In a letter sent to a friend just before his death, Christy wrote that although he was full of dread and despair for the future, perhaps he might 'become notorious again just for the hell of it'. He was depending on his last novel to do this, but it was not *A Promising Career* that would again make Christy a celebrity. Instead, it would be the film version of his first small memoir, *My Left Foot*.

Chapter Thirteen

A FILM

A bit of light between this melancholy missive, next spring my new novel A Promising Career comes out in Britain and the States – you will accept a signed copy just for old time's sake? As you know, it took me almost five insufferable years and 3 drafts to complete, and I was seriously on the point of flinging it in the fire, but then I decided I had damn all to lose so I sent it to my publishers on impulse, and was genuinely astounded by their response – they say it's the best thing I've done to date and predict great things for it, even talking in terms of a best-seller and other heady stuff. I never quite lost faith in it during all that time, but was completely flummoxed by S and W's [Secker & Warburg's] ecstatic reaction and the huge advance they gave me. I don't know if it's my best novel yet, but at least the fucking thing is being published and that's the main thing.

I'm also working on a new collection of poems called INMATES which might appear at the same time; all rather sombre and a bit on the dark-side centring round my various sojourns in the aforementioned 'mental hotels', but occasionally injected with flashes of impish if macabre humour and some surreal insights into my 'guardians'.

So, you see poor old Brown hasn't quite become a cabbage yet and might even become notorious again just for the hell of it.

Christy Brown, writing to Bill O'Donnell,
26 August 1981,
two weeks before his death.

When Noel Pearson was working as Christy Brown's agent in Dublin in the 1970s, the two of them had discussed making a film of *Down All the Days*. Noel had asked Christy who he thought should play him; Christy told him he felt Marlon Brando was perfect for the part. Pearson laughed but Christy was totally serious. Fifteen years later, in 1988, Pearson sat in New York thinking of a way to put Christy's life on film. He was working in the theatre, producing a show with the American actor Caroll O'Connor (who was famous for playing Archie Bunker in a long-running and popular television show in the United States called *All in the Family*).

Pearson had always wanted to make *Down All the Days* into a film; just as Kevin McClory had imagined it would in 1970, Noel was also convinced the novel would translate well onto film. But, Pearson recalls, Christy's editor and friend, David Farrer (who, like Noel, sometimes acted as his agent), had sold the rights to 'a boyfriend' (he was a cameraman working in the British television company Channel 4). The rights to *Down All the Days* were sold in perpetuity and therefore the film could never be made without the cameraman's permission; what is more, the rights could never be bought from him. Noel was frustrated by this. It seems David Farrer, acting as Christy's agent, publisher and friend, had at some stage taken advantage of him. *Down All the Days* was discussed by several producers at the time of its publication as an adaptable book for film. How and when Christy sold the rights to Farrer and in what circumstances is unknown, but it left Pearson in a difficult position. He knew and admired Christy and felt his story was something that ought to be dramatised.

As Pearson sat in his office in New York, he picked up a copy of *My Left Foot* and decided to read it again (having read it in the '70s). After finishing it, he thought to himself: 'This is better than *Down All the Days*. This is much simpler. This is less purply.' He realised it was perfect for film because of its simplicity, its visual quality and straightforward narrative.

Down All the Days, with its prolix prose, wild imagery and lyrical language, was too complicated and detailed to make into a film, although later Shane Connaughton, the Irish writer, actor and screenwriter who co-wrote the script for *My Left Foot*, would say that there was still a film to be made from *Down All the Days*. But Pearson had spotted an opportunity, and his instinct, which had for years been honed working with and managing the music group The Dubliners and working in theatre in Dublin and New York, told him he was on to a good thing. Also, the play he was producing was not doing well, and so his mind turned to the idea of making *My Left Foot* into a film.

As Pearson starting thinking about making the film, he wondered to himself who he knew who could write a treatment (a basic outline explaining the film's plot). At that stage in his career, as he says himself, he 'didn't even know what a treatment was'. Indeed, Noel knew very little about film-making. A few months after his New York show with Carroll had closed, he was back in Dublin. He sat in a pub drinking with his friend the actor Alan Devlin, telling him about the project and how he wanted to make a film of Christy Brown's life. He asked Devlin if he knew anyone he thought might be able and willing to write a treatment and then the script for the film. Just down the road, Shane Connaughton was deciding whether or not he should go for a drink in the same pub to meet a few friends who were involved in the theatre. He decided no and then he changed his mind and decided yes. He walked into the pub where Devlin and Pearson were discussing who could write *My Left Foot*. At that exact moment, Alan said to Noel, 'Shane Connaughton, he could write for you – sure, look, there he is.' Pearson waved Connaughton over and bought him a drink. As Connaughton remembers it, it was a complete fluke – one which landed him an Oscar nomination.

Jim Sheridan was a friend of Devlin's, and the actor had mentioned Sheridan's name to Pearson as someone who might be helpful in the writing of the film. After Pearson had spoken with Connaughton in Dublin, and asked him to start working on the treatment and script (which Connaughton said he was happy to do), Pearson went back to New York and, following Devlin's advice, decided to meet with Jim about the project. Jim and he were friends, and they had spent quite a bit of time together. When they met, Pearson said to Sheridan, 'I'm gonna make a film of *My Left Foot*. I don't know how, but I'm gonna make it.' He told him he had asked Shane Connaughton to start working on the script, and Sheridan said he was friendly with Connaughton and that he really wanted to be a part of it. After all, as his brother Peter said, he knew there was potential in *My Left Foot*, and now his words – 'There's a fucking story in there and I'm gonna do it' – had come to fruition.

Connaughton wrote a few drafts and then Pearson brought in Sheridan – he thought they would make a good team. Noel put the two men in an office he had on Dawson Street in Dublin with a copy of *My Left Foot* and locked the door, 'literally'. Connaughton remembers that he and Sheridan had wonderful fun writing the script. Pearson's office was full of 'big cardboard boxes full of cheque-book stubs – stacks as big as a chair – it was fantastic'. As Sheridan put it: 'I wrote the first thirty pages and Shane contradicted me for sixty and I contradicted him for the last thirty and everyone loved it. We wrote the first draft very quickly and then Shane did a second draft and I did a third draft and that's basically how it went.'

Connaughton and Sheridan were annoyed that they could not use *Down All the Days*, which, Shane says, 'was a handicap ... because all the best stuff, all the best scenes and all the best writing are in *Down All the Days*.' Jim said when interviewed, 'I always thought that *My Left Foot* was a very simple, heartfelt story and *Down All the Days* was more like Thomas Wolfe, and is just flying all over the place and very variable. I think we were lucky in a way that the rights to that weren't available and we had to just cobble it together from little bits of facts about his life.' In the end, both Connaughton and Sheridan felt they had succeeded in staying true to the spirit of Christy Brown, although they reworked some scenes from the book, elaborated on others and invented some.

Pearson now needed a director for the film and an actor to play the part of Christy. No one in the industry wanted either job. Noel, Jim and Shane went to London several times to meet various directors (including John McColgan of Tyrone Productions, who would later direct the Riverdance show), and, according to Connaughton, at every meeting Sheridan was seething with fury: 'We went to London to meet a director, who had been an actor. We went to this restaurant in Soho, and all I could see was that Jim hated being in the presence of this man. It was *so* painfully obvious.' Jim was desperate to direct it, he concedes: 'I wanted to make the movie and all the people I met to direct it had different ideas. To begin with, Richard Harris was supposed to be one of the directors. We met in the Berkeley Court Hotel, and he wanted me to change the script and start with the birth of Christy and not have a flashback. He said flashbacks were old-fashioned. I refused to rewrite it, even though I was impoverished, you know . . . I had no money. I remember Richard saying to me, "God, you're arrogant."'

After one meeting, Jim got down on his knees in the middle of Soho and begged Pearson to let him be the director of *My Left Foot*. Noel looked down on him and replied, 'Look, Jim, I'm not letting you direct it. Sure, even RTÉ wouldn't touch you with a bargepole.' Pearson says, 'He was desperate to direct it. He nearly drove me mad.' Eventually, after several discussions, he told Sheridan he could direct the film. But they had no principal actor.

Pearson remembers, 'We couldn't get anyone . . . you know, lots of people passed on it. I think it was at my house, I was with Daniel Day-Lewis and some friends having drinks, and I was talking about the project and what was going on. I told Daniel this story [Christy Brown's life story] at three o'clock in the morning.

'No one would do it. I had only told Daniel the story and didn't think he would do it. And I needed someone to play the part. Then later, I was with Tom Hickey, I think we were in a pub, and he said, "Fuck it . . . send it to him [Day-Lewis] anyway." So we sent it. He came back in two days. He said when he was reading it, he thought to himself, "I've heard this story somewhere before," and then he looked at the front and saw my name on it and remembered when I was telling him the story in my house. He had thought at the time, "When is this geezer gonna offer me the job?"'

'That's how it all started . . . I think the great thing about it was we had no ambitions for it at all. Just so long as it got on in Dublin. That's all. It only cost a million seven. But there was something about it. First of all, Daniel Day-Lewis was extraordinary, so was Ray McAnally and so were they all. The casting was great.'

Connaughton felt the same way: 'You don't really know when you put on a play or make a film how it's going to go; it really is in the lap of the gods. The best thing to do is expect nothing and then you're always surprised. I mean, Cavan will never win the All-Ireland football final in my lifetime – but maybe they will, and won't I be pleasantly surprised?'

Before Day-Lewis came onto the set, he spent over six weeks attending the cerebral palsy clinic where Christy had received therapy. Although the location was different, as were the treatments (which were far advanced from when Christy had been diagnosed), he did absorb the same atmosphere and tried to gain a deeper understanding of the emotional and physical effects of suffering from an illness like double athetoid cerebral palsy. In fact, Day-Lewis ended up working with Dr Sheehan. In her notes, which she donated to the National Library of Ireland, Sheehan wrote:

It was an odd quirk of fate that when the film of 'My Left Foot' was being made at Ardmore Studios, I was asked to advise and to teach Daniel Day-Lewis, who was playing the part of Christy Brown, how to speak with dysarthria, when most of my life I have spent trying to make people with dysarthria speak normally.

The director, producer and cinematographer on *My Left Foot* embarked on making a feature film, which was something none of them had done before. Day-Lewis had taken lead roles only in *My Beautiful Laundrette* and *The Unbearable Lightness of Being*, so he was relatively inexperienced when he came to play Christy Brown. However, the supporting cast he had around him was very strong. Brenda Fricker played Christy's mother, Ray McAnally played his father, Patrick, and Fiona Shaw's character was a composite of Katriona Maguire, Dr Robert Collis and Dr Patricia Sheehan.

Connaughton had worked with Ray McAnally many years before the making of *My Left Foot*, playing Macduff to McAnally's Macbeth. They rehearsed their fight scenes early in the morning in Dublin's Abbey Theatre, and one day they started talking about religion. Shane turned to Ray and said, 'Well, you don't really believe all of that do you, Ray?' Ray brought him to the window of the Abbey, pointed down to St Mary's Pro-Cathedral on Marlborough Street and said, 'Do you see that? That's the Pro-Cathedral. And in there there's a tabernacle. And in that tabernacle is the sacred host. And I believe that is the body of Christ more than I believe in you standing in front of me.' Shane was shocked; although he was from Cavan, he had always worked in the theatre in England and had never heard an actor speaking in those terms.

Ray McAnally's performance as Patrick Brown in *My Left Foot* was too intense and frightening for most viewers; Pearson says most people who saw the film afterwards thought of Ray as a hard, hard man. McAnally had read Christy's play *The Hotel*, and so he had an inside perspective that not many others had on Christy's family life. At the time of his performance in *My Left Foot*, McAnally was at the height of his powers. He was a magnificent actor who was mature and had experience in the theatre and in film, and he was poised after playing Patrick Brown to become a major film star. As Connaughton remembers, 'He had done what every actor wants to do, he had done it, he'd made a huge impact and was getting oodles of work from America and everything. He had cracked it, he was huge, and everyone was lining up to give him parts.' Tragically, McAnally died of a heart attack on 15 June 1989, just after the film found success in America.

Later, producers and directors in major Hollywood studios would admit privately to Pearson and Connaughton that they couldn't have made the film in the United States. They would have sentimentalised it; as an old saying in the studios goes, 'We love this; now let's fuck it up.' Fortunately, the cast and crew of *My Left Foot* didn't have that problem. As Pearson says, no big studio heads were overseeing the production, no unions were involved and a tremendous *esprit de corps* pushed the writers, actors and director to produce some of their best work. Jim Sheridan's talent for working closely with actors in tight spaces began to emerge. As Connaughton says, '*My Left Foot* is quite a crude piece of work in a way. It's strange; its strength is Jim working with actors in a film – I mean, nobody is better than him.' Ulick O'Connor, who worked on the set, feels that: 'He [Christy] will last for three reasons: he'll last mainly for the book [*Down All the Days*], he'll last for what he did himself and he'll last for the film. Jim did a great thing. It is just amazing – he'd got Christy.'

O'Connor remembers playing an art critic in a scene that recreated Christy's exhibition at the Agnew Somerville Gallery. 'What we all want to know, Christy, is can you use your middle leg?' he shouted out as an improvisation. Shane Connaughton felt the line ought not to have been cut.

As O'Connor observed Day-Lewis in character, he was

astonished by him: 'I think it is probably one of the great performances in the history of the movies. When I came down to see the film, I saw Daniel. At seven in the morning, he started to talk like Christy, and he talked like Christy all day, every day. At four o'clock in the afternoon [after spending the day on the set], I was waiting for a taxi with Daniel. I might as well have been standing beside a shadow because he was gone, there was nothing in him – nothing there at all. Daniel Day-Lewis was just an empty shell and gradually, gradually he would become a human being again. But he gave everything in that performance. Having known Christy and having watched Daniel playing him is the most extraordinary thing I have ever seen. I knew it was one of the few great performances, like Orson Welles [in *Citizen Kane*] or Olivier [in *Richard III*].'

Day-Lewis famously stayed in character while on set for the six weeks that the film was being shot. One day, his agent, Julian Belfrage, came to visit him at Ardmore Studios in Bray, County Wicklow, and to take him to lunch. Pearson told him, 'You know, Julian, he is in character.'

'Fuck off, the silly bugger,' Belfrage replied.

'No, he is,' Pearson told him.

Belfrage and Day-Lewis went to lunch but Daniel wouldn't come out of character. The agent was furious and told Day-Lewis to 'piss off, fuck off and get a bit of sense', commenting that, 'When John Hurt did *The Elephant Man*, he didn't behave like this.'

Ann cried as she watched Day-Lewis being fed at Ardmore Studios during the making of the film. She had spent years feeding Christy herself, and the similarity between the actor and her brother moved her to tears. She had to leave the studio after seeing him for only a few minutes. Later, Daniel apologised for upsetting her, explaining simply that he was trying to do the best he could. Ann was amazed at the work he put into his acting. She says, 'I looked after Christy for five years, after our mother died. When I saw the film, I cried. I think because Daniel, he was Christy. I remember being on the set and Daniel didn't get out of costume, he stayed as Christy. It was very emotional to see; for instance, Daniel getting fed, it was too much, really, and then to see the film . . . Daniel never came out of character, never.

'There was one day when I was watching him being fed, and I was so moved, because I had to do that for Christy. I had to leave the table I was that upset. A while later, Daniel came up to me and said he was sorry if he upset me . . . well, I have to say, it was very upsetting to go out on the set . . . It was so real that it was Christy sitting there, you know. It was very, very emotional. And I said, I wouldn't need to hack this, I couldn't come out here again.

'Not that day, another time we met, I can't remember, it was before the premiere anyway, and I was saying to him what I'm saying to you now, it really was very emotional, and he'd said, "I'm very sorry but I couldn't get out of character or I wouldn't be able to get back into it. I never meant to hurt you." It wouldn't be his nature, but that's the way he was. He was a lovely man, great craic to be with. There was some debate at the time that Christy should have been played by a handicapped person, but no, I don't think so, I don't think they would have captured Christy the way Daniel did.

'He did research from that *Radharc* film [the 1962 RTÉ documentary on Christy], and he got all the facial expressions from that. I was never on a film set in my life. When we went down to see this room, he had every photograph I know of Christy. Blown up and all. They had to keep all these things on the wall to make sure they got all the facial expressions; he had all the videos and all, like over the years, and you'd say to yourself, "God, I can remember that."

'We went for a drink with Daniel to the Stone Boat and we met all the cast; we met Brenda Fricker a few times, but she didn't come to my house. She was very nice. I thought she portrayed my mother quite well. She got a little bit of her across, not a lot, but a little. Then again, they had nothing to copy from. There was loads of footage of Christy over the years. Brenda was good.'

Of the film, Katriona Maguire says, 'Well, the character in the film was a composite of myself, Dr Sheehan and Dr Collis. Fiona Shaw was good, marvellous, and Brenda Fricker was fantastic. You know, I knew Christy's mother so well and she was one of the most memorable women I have ever met, a remarkable woman. Daniel Day-Lewis did deserve an Oscar; you know, there were three Oscars for that film, which was made on a shoestring. But it's not a documentary; it's fiction, really – based on fact. Daniel Day-Lewis was wonderful, just wonderful. Interestingly enough, at the premiere of the film in the Savoy in Dublin, Daniel Day-Lewis came out all on his own and nobody knew him, and now I think he'd be lionised if he walked out of a cinema. I just walked over and said to him, "I think you've done a wonderful job on Christy." But they had no idea in Ireland that the film was going to be so successful . . . you know, it was extraordinary for this country to win three Oscars with that film.'

Disabled artists and actors complained that Day-Lewis had been chosen to play Christy, when they felt that a disabled actor should have been given the part. But for Ann, there was no one else who could have played her brother. She says, 'Even with the speech impediment that Daniel had, it came across like you could understand it. I did a programme for Channel 4 about a year later; they came out here [to Ann's home] and they did it. They told me that people were saying why didn't they use a disabled person? And I said I've nothing against a disabled person but, I said, Christy's speech impediment was that bad I had to interpret for him if you were coming out to interview him. So I said they couldn't do that in film. They had to have someone who had a slight speech impediment but that the audience would understand.'

For Ann and the rest of Christy's family, Daniel Day-Lewis became Christy Brown. Some of them felt when they saw him, both in the flesh and on screen, that they were seeing a ghost. The Browns were very close to Daniel and remember him on set as frighteningly committed to the part but retaining his sense of humour. One day, Christy's younger brother Francis laughed as he said to him, 'Ah now, Daniel, if you're really in character, maybe I should help you to the toilet. After all, that's how Christy did it, and if you really are going to stay in character … well, we'd be more than happy to help.' 'F-f-f-fuck off,' Day-Lewis replied in Christy's voice, and they both laughed.

In one scene in particular, set in a restaurant after Christy has just had his first art exhibition, Day-Lewis managed to capture Christy's temper and vituperative tongue. In the scene, Christy, in frustration and furious with jealousy over the engagement of Fiona Shaw's character Dr Cole, drinks several whiskeys in a row and replies to one character who tells him to calm down, 'If you don't shut up, I will kick you in the only place on your body which is animated.' When Cole's fiancé, played by Adrian Dunbar, attempts to remove Christy from the table at which the group is sat, Day-Lewis chose to grab the tablecloth with his teeth in protest. The scene is incredibly painful to watch, and a very accurate portrait of the ferocious temper Christy sometimes displayed. Dunbar remembers, 'I saw the script and I was offered this part. Jim had seen me in a play and offered me a part in the film, so I said yes, fantastic, I love the script. And when it was being made, when we did the scene in the restaurant where he [Day-Lewis] freaks out, it was really … it was uncomfortable, it was scary. It is a big scene. It was just the take – you just go with what's gonna happen; it was great. It was really, really emotional. We were outside after the scene and Jim said, "What do you think?" and I says, "If 10 per cent of what's happening gets onto the screen, it's just gonna be amazing."'

The famous film critic Pauline Kael would later watch *My*

Left Foot as the film did the awards rounds in America. She found the restaurant incident in the film 'one of the most emotionally wrenching scenes I've ever experienced in the movies'. In the same review, she said Day-Lewis as Christy recalled 'Olivier's crookbacked, long-nosed Richard III. Day-Lewis's Christy Brown has all the sexual seductiveness that was so startling in the Olivier Richard.'

When Noel Pearson was told that the performance was quite terrifying in its accuracy, he replied, 'Oh, it's scary all right. But, you see, I used to take him [Day-Lewis] up almost every Sunday morning to the Stone Boat in Crumlin. He is very shrewd. Every Sunday, we would sit around and after they [the locals] knew it was free drink, there'd be loads of people there. The last time we went down, there must have been twenty of them, and that's how he got the accent. We went there every Sunday morning for about six weeks. They thought Daniel would be a "British boy", and after all the Troubles in the '70s and with the accent and all, they kept saying, "How's this guy gonna play our Christy?"'

Although the Brown family were pleased with the result of the film, certain things they found laughable, such as a scene in which Bridget carries the young Christy (played by Hugh O'Connor) up the stairs of the family home. As the late Mona Byrne put it, 'My mother . . . they had her portrayed as bringing Christy up the stairs on her own. How in the name of God could she do that? She never had to do that. She done an awful lot for him, but she never had to do that. There was just no way that would have happened.'

She continued, 'Another thing: my father was fond of the drink, but then there was a lot of frustration. We're talking about Ireland. He used to come up every morning and take Christy out of bed, and he would always wash him and shave him, give my mother a hand. Daddy did that every morning. He never once encouraged one of his sons or anyone in the family to drink with him. Putting Christy on his shoulder,

"He's a Brown" – no such thing. I mean, so far-fetched, really and truly. It didn't do us any favours but, at the same time, it was a great achievement to see your brother up in lights. It was a great encouragement to other disabled people.'

The Browns understood that it was fiction, not fact. Day-Lewis's performance particularly gave them great faith in their cooperation on the set; they thought the film was an authentic representation of the brother they loved so much.

When the film was finished, cut and ready to be shown, Pearson decided to enter it into the Cannes Film Festival. A high-up official at the film festival refused, telling Pearson, 'How can we ask people in black ties and full dress to come and watch a guy drooling on himself in a wheelchair?' Pearson decided to have it screened privately at Cannes, and that is when the buzz about the profundity of the film and the shocking quality of Day-Lewis's performance began. At the first screening there were seventy-five people watching in chairs and seventy-five on the floor, then at the next screening there were two hundred there, and then three hundred. Through word of mouth, *My Left Foot* became the film to see at Cannes. Another stroke of luck would change the course of the history of Christy Brown and his story. Simply by accident, Harvey Weinstein walked into one of those screenings. He and his brother were just starting Miramax Films and had gone to Cannes because they were intent upon finding small art-house films to promote in the United States. They believed they could break into new territory by taking risks and by bringing unique and intelligent films to mass audiences. Their idea would be a great success and Miramax Films would become an enormously powerful production company. Weinstein had gone to Cannes to see and perhaps purchase as the beginning of his company a small film that won the Palme d'Or award: *Sex, Lies, and Videotape*. However, his keen nose for a film with potential led him to go and see the picture everyone was talking about: *My Left Foot*.

Chapter Fourteen

AN OSCAR

It was good to get your telegram. I was so happy not to
leave, to return to Ireland and the Browns, empty-handed –
All good wishes
Daniel D.L.

Daniel Day-Lewis, writing to Seán Brown,
March 1989

Originally, the cast and crew of the film and the Brown family all thought *My Left Foot* might do well at home and possibly in Britain. Pearson had acquired funding from private investors and from Granada Films. But after the success at Cannes, he realised he might have a big hit on his hands, and he took the film to the *Los Angeles Times* film critic, Shelia Benson, who told him it had 'Oscar' written all over it. The reviews were sensational. As *My Left Foot* began to do the rounds of nominations for awards in preparation for the Oscars, the news was fantastic. Benson wrote, 'This is the one you see for the pure love of film-making. It's tough-minded, unsentimental and ferociously brilliant acting.' *The New York Times* called the film 'an intelligent and beautifully acted adaptation' while *Rolling Stone* said, 'Day-Lewis gives a towering performance – fierce, witty and moving . . . *My Left Foot*, a keen match of actor and subject, stands as an eloquent tribute to the talents of both.'

Pearson rang Granada to tell them that they were all on to a winner. Granada told him that while he had been talking with Benson about how the film was a dead cert for the Oscars, Harvey Weinstein had called from a toilet in London's Heathrow airport. He had bought the rights to the film outside the United Kingdom and Ireland just before he boarded a flight back to Los Angeles. Although Noel was disappointed because he wasn't able to obtain the rights himself, in retrospect he sees Weinstein as a tremendous businessman who loves film, and he 'thought Harvey did a fantastic marketing job'.

Pearson and Sheridan went to live in Los Angeles for weeks before the Academy Awards. When they arrived, Pearson asked Weinstein, 'How does the Oscar thing work?' According to Pearson, the Oscars are 'like a Fianna Fáil election'. The older actors who are established in the Academy of Motion Picture Arts and Sciences often give parties at the expense of a host who has a film in the running for an award. People talk, stories are told and all the clichés about schmoozing, it seems, are true. Still, Weinstein and Pearson were not selling just any old film – or any old performance. Jim Sheridan 'knew Daniel Day-Lewis was amazing as Christy, I knew that at least the performance would be spoken about; but getting five nominations was a big surprise, you know, it was great.'

Day-Lewis's portrayal of Christy gained him eleven major award nominations worldwide. He won in the best actor category at the Academy Awards, the New York Film Critics Circle Awards, the LA Film Critics Association Awards, the European Film Awards, the Montreal World Film Festival, the London Critics' Circle Film Awards, the Golden Globes and the US National Society of Film Critics Awards. When Day-Lewis won his Oscar, he smiled, said very simply to the audience, 'I would like to say thank you to Christy Brown,' and left the stage.

In Los Angeles during the run-up to the ceremony, Pearson, Sheridan and Connaughton all worked hard at promoting the film. Disability became a major issue in the media, as Tom Cruise was also nominated for his portrayal of someone with a disability: Ron Kovic, the Vietnam veteran returning home in Oliver Stone's film *Born on the Fourth of July*. Pearson comments, 'The irony of the whole thing was, the film that we were fighting all the way – they had best actor, best director and best film nominations – was *Born on the Fourth of July*. They couldn't believe that Daniel had beaten Tom Cruise, 'cause he was the "golden boy". They kept putting up ramps when they showed the films . . . A lot of people thought Christy Brown was still alive but they were for the guy who wrote *Fourth of July*.'

Tom Cruise was, at that stage, at the height of his career; but Day-Lewis's performance had left many people wondering if he would win. *My Left Foot* was also nominated for best director and best film, as well as for best actress and best screenplay. Studios were amazed by the film. Someone told Pearson, 'Christ, you've got a Rocky Balboa in a wheelchair on your hands!'

Protests began as people in wheelchairs found that although disability had become a topic of debate in the media, few cinemas were providing appropriate access for disabled people to see the films that had been nominated for Oscars. Christy Brown and his disability had been hijacked before in order to create headlines. In 1983, the abortion issue and the debate as to whether or not it should be legalised was raging in Ireland, and many letters poured into the Irish newspapers using his life as an argument for the pro-life position. Journalists and the public alike wrote that most women would have aborted a child like Christy, and look what he did with his life. Christy would have despised his life being used as any kind of platform, but as far as the success of the film was concerned, his friends and family are confident that he would have been pleased. Imagining Christy's reaction to his life being made into a film, Katriona says, 'I can just see the twinkle in his eye – he would have loved it.'

The success of the film of *My Left Foot* changed the fortunes of all the artists involved in the project, including Christy Brown. Shane Connaughton remembers how surreal it was to be invited (as is almost everyone who is nominated for an Oscar) to see all the major studio heads in Hollywood after the success of the film and how they responded to his work. He recalls walking into rooms with men in suits who exchanged pleasantries and asked him about his work. He carried with him a copy of the book he had just finished, and the reaction he repeatedly received when they saw his novel was 'Wow, this guy is a *real* writer'; it was as though they had never met someone who had written a book before.

In all, the film was nominated for thirty-one film awards and received sixteen. As Pearson says, 'It was a great thing. The film was made partly as a homage to Christy. He was such an inspirational kind of a guy. I mean, we moan about a toothache, so I think that's why it worked . . . apart from all the Oscars and all that, he [Christy] did a tremendous amount for disability, 'cause he encouraged a lot of kids, and a lot of men. He never saw himself as disabled . . . he had an amazing spirit, that's what he had. Jim Sheridan had a great description of him, you know – that he was like a 747 that would take off but he couldn't get into the sky, because of his disability.

'There was this kind of naivety in making the film that had a pure energy that you can't get unless there's something driving you, and that's what made the film. It was such a moment in Irish film and theatre. Nobody should ever try and take it on, like they did try to take it on with a film called *Inside I'm Dancing*. You can't compete with Daniel Day-Lewis's performance. But the problem is when you do a film like that, everything is downhill afterwards. You just gotta keep going. Innocence, you know.'

The award-winning playwright and professor of creative writing at University College Dublin, Frank McGuinness (author of *Observe the Sons of Ulster Marching Towards the*

Somme and who adapted Brian Friel's *Dancing at Lughnasa* for film), comments that the film was in some ways a curse to Christy: 'Christy Brown got an immense amount of publicity from the film, which did a lot of good, but it could have done a lot of harm as well. You know, he is so identified with that magnificent performance now and that is possibly why Christy's work is not read as widely as it might have been.' In other words, when people think of Christy, they think of Day-Lewis's towering performance and not of the artist and his work.

McGuinness also says of Christy, 'He is an exceptional writer, there is no question of that. He is such a good poet. I think the poems and the letters, some of which are glorious, should be published together. Of course, *Down All the Days* will last forever, but he did keep some of his best writing for his letters. You must remember, as Noel Pearson says, and by God he means it, there's no such thing as a free lunch. Christy Brown got a tremendous amount of publicity from the film. The film got so much recognition and inevitably in this world of pros and cons, a lot of his work will be devalued to some extent or underestimated because of the scale of exposure the film got. In the scheme of things, *My Left Foot* should have been a small Irish movie that did well here and died in London and was discovered twenty years later as a masterpiece, but instead it defied all conventional wisdom, and Christy would have approved.

'I certainly remember him [Christy Brown]. I was about seventeen or eighteen when it [*Down All the Days*] came out. I read it when I was about twenty. It always reminded me of "Strawberry Fields Forever", *Down All the Days* – "let me take you down . . .", that was the kind of connection I was making with it. I never thought they would make it into a film but it was an important book when it came out.

'I think these [letters and poems] deserve, as I said, to be in print. But the play [*Mrs Brennan*], compared to the rest of the writing, well, he is not a playwright. He can certainly do dialogue in his books, but in the play, it's overdone, it just falls apart. I feel it is just not his gift. It's just that some people are good writing plays and some people are good writing poems; that's the law of the land. Some people are good at football, some people play tennis. Plays are very hard to write; while Christy's lyricism is marvellously rich, deep, broad, touching, if you look at the most lyrical poet of twentieth-century theatre, Tennessee Williams, and examine his plays, it's shocking how spare they are, how careful Williams is in what he lets people say. I don't think Christy Brown had this gift, or he certainly couldn't develop it. But go back to the fiction, the poetry, the correspondence. The time is right for looking at him as a writer: forget the person, forget the singing, forget getting drunk, forget that.'

The author Brian Lynch feels Jim Sheridan makes films about 'what it is to be Irish' and 'what Ireland is; what it is to be the working man in Ireland'. The actor Adrian Dunbar agrees with him and thinks Sheridan and Pearson were the only people who could have turned Christy's life into a film, because they knew and understood working-class Dublin. Dunbar believes only Sheridan and Pearson would have been brave enough to make a film about a working-class disabled writer like Christy Brown. They were not looking for awards or success; as Jim Sheridan had told his brother in 1981, after the play of *Down All the Days* was shut down in two weeks after three years of work, there *was* 'a fucking great story there', and both of them knew it.

The culture of Ireland knows what it is to be marginalised and silenced, like Christy. The language of Ireland was banned by the English for hundreds of years. Irish sports, Irish writing and Irish songs were all made illegal at certain stages when Ireland was under British rule. The language that is spoken today in Ireland is charming and unusual to people who do not come from there; there is a simple reason for this.

The Irish language disappeared as the English (and their language) ruled the nation, and Irish people had to learn English very quickly in order to survive. An expression such as 'I do be going to the shop' (which would often be used in Ireland today) is in fact perfectly correct grammatically in the Irish language, but when transposed to English sounds ridiculous. Hence the great character of the stage Irishman, who often drinks too much and speaks in an idiosyncratic way. As Professor Declan Kiberd points out in his essay 'The Fall of the Stage Irishman' (1979), even Shakespeare used a stage Irishman to create a laugh in his work (in *Henry V*). For centuries, Ireland's national identity and culture were fractured.

Sheridan and Pearson, like Joyce, reinvented what stories should or could be told. Reflecting on the film, Sheridan says, 'When you are making a film, you have to put yourself in the main character.' The success of *My Left Foot* surprised no one more than Sheridan or Pearson. Like Behan and Christy before them, they were familiar with the trappings of the stage Irish cliché, and how it could be retold and reworked. Theirs was the first Irish film made in Ireland about an Irishman with an Irish cast and crew. Their determination to be honest to the spirit of Christy and to simply make a good film, as opposed to trying to win awards or please critics, allowed them to do all those things. What they also did was breathe life into Irish film-making.

Day-Lewis's performance left a legacy that is difficult for any act to follow. His commitment to creating a character who was as true to life as possible made for a legendary figure being put on celluloid. This left Christy Brown's literature behind in its wake. Day-Lewis's performance and the inventiveness of Sheridan and Pearson were not the only reasons the film was so successful. As a narrative, Christy Brown's life is an unbeatable story, with its dramatic twists and turns; his work, on the other hand, and its exploration of the uncomfortable places most people do not like to go – depression, isolation and physical suffering – is more difficult to love. As Dunbar says of Christy's work, 'It has that thing of feeling that you don't belong. Ultimately, there are certain doors closed to you in society because you are disabled; this is the thing that informs his [Christy's] experience of the world. He sees it through that filter.

'With writers like Christy and Brendan, people are scared of them because they tell the truth. With Brendan, you had a scenario where he put ordinary people on the stage for the first time and had them talk about big stuff; up until that point only educated people talked about big stuff. Brendan achieved quite a bit in his life and no one has called him "Brendan the genius"; obviously because if you start calling Christy and Brendan geniuses, what's the point? Nobody gets to feel good about it except the Dublin working classes. Brendan came along and he had ordinary people talk about things like the death penalty on stage, and have an opinion about it, which was tough – especially in the UK in the 1960s.

'My theory is you don't hear about people who the institutions cannot feel good about; which is why we have to put up with mediocrity a lot of the time, because they are elevating minor figures to major places. Geniuses open up ideas. You very rarely see people come through who have come from nowhere, because that's the nature of the institution. It likes to pat itself on the back.

'Where is Christy? He's a bit like Percy French, Tom Lehrer – people who have been kept alive in popular folk culture. People remember. Folk culture was big in Ireland because we didn't have the Industrial Revolution. The Industrial Revolution destroyed folk culture.

'But Christy is there in Dublin. The people who he cared for – that constituency – will never forget him. Both Behan and Christy, they knew that because they were not part of the establishment, they would not be properly recognised. Where do you go from there? You rely on the fact that maybe in twenty years' time a taxi driver from your constituency might do something.'

Chapter Fifteen

AN ENDING

Yes, the news of Paddy Kavanagh's death did indeed reach me – not through my own knowledge, for I never read the newspapers except rarely – but Beth read about it and told me. I was sorry to hear it – which you might not believe from the little bit of a poem which I wrote on hearing the sad news and which I am enclosing, but I believe in being honest and true to one's feelings even in respect to the dead, and my poem is sincere as any that will doubtless be written in his memory . . . Kavanagh must be honoured and nobly remembered, instead of putting one of those stupid bloody plaques to his memory, which seems about the limit to which Ireland goes to honour her eminent men and women. I hope they do something real and practical and of lasting benefit instead, like constructing a Kavanagh Library or a poetry scholarship system as they did eventually with Yeats.

Christy Brown, writing to Katriona Maguire,
30 November 1967

In September 2004, I put up a plaque at Christy Brown's home on Stannaway Road in Kimmage. I nominated Christy as an artist who deserved his family home to be recognised as an important cultural landmark by simply writing to the Dublin Tourism Board and explaining why he deserved such an honour. For me, getting the plaque at 54 Stannaway Road was a way to thank his family for all the help they had given me in the writing of my Masters dissertation in 2003, while I was studying at University College Dublin. The journalists who came to 54 Stannaway Road later wrote of how good it was to know that things were still the same down in Kimmage, that everyone headed off to the pub afterwards. Nothing was written of Christy's contribution to art and literature. Instead, the newspapers described his childhood in the slums and his disability and referenced Day-Lewis's portrayal of him in 1988.

It still perplexes me why Christy has been forgotten as an artist. In his poetry (all of which is now out of print) and his prose, his skills as a writer are vast. While conducting research, I was shocked to contact the National Archives in Dublin and find that the original copy of *My Left Foot* was held in their medical section rather than with the other 'literary' books. The famous nineteenth-century Danish philosopher and theologian Søren Kierkegaard said, 'Once you label me, you negate me.' What you judge, you cannot understand. Understanding comes only through observation.

In observing his work, rather than judging it as something written by someone with his left foot, I have found themes of the Gothic, a strong sense of violence, an eye for understanding human detail and a deep understanding of the commodification of Ireland. His aesthetic is complex and interesting and deserves to be looked at. It seems to me that the more Christy articulated himself, the more pain he was in. He was an individualist, a democratic thinker, anti-Church, sexual and open-minded. What is so exciting about his work is that it is waiting to be explored and evaluated.

Christy discovered the work of W.H. Auden at the end of his life, a sadness he expresses in his poem 'W.H. Auden':

> ... I yet know only half your mind
> half of the world you made uniquely your own
> and the other half beckons like an unexplored country
> wherein I shall falter often early and late

be confused and befuddled by so many trails lured by
   signs that apparently lead into nowhere
save that the nowhere you inhabited teemed with such
   life
as to leave me panting and many times lost
in my belated crusade to find you –
   Christy Brown.

SELECT BIBLIOGRAPHY AND SOURCES

UNPUBLISHED SOURCES

This biography draws on the papers of Christy Brown – a collection of letters, unpublished writings, sketches and paintings which have not previously been brought to light and have not yet been catalogued. The book also draws on interviews with those who knew or admired Christy. All interviews (listed below) were conducted by the author.

INTERVIEWS

Banville, John, personal interview (9 March 2007)

Brown, Eamonn, personal interview (18 May 2006)

Brown, Francis, personal interviews (28 March and 1 June 2006)

Brown, Paddy and Betty, personal interviews (29 October and 6 December 2004)

Brown, Seán, and Kelvin Moyses, personal interviews (14 March 2003, 21 December 2004, 21 and 22 December 2005, 11 January and 27 December 2006)

Byrne, Mona, personal interview (20 January 2003)

Connaughton, Shane, personal interview (9 February 2006)

Drew, Ronnie, personal interview (12 July 2006)

Dunbar, Adrian, personal interview (5 January 2007)

Jones, Ann, personal interviews (16 January 2003, 15 December and 18 December 2004)

Jordan, Anthony, personal interview (14 February 2006)

Liddy, James, personal interview (22 March 2006)

Lynch, Brian, personal interview (19 January 2006)

Maguire, Katriona, personal interviews (14 July 2003, 13 December 2004, 1 November 2005)

Mahon, Maura, personal interview (21 February 2006)

McGuinness, Frank, personal interview (20 July 2006)

O'Connor, Ulick, personal interviews (10 March and 7 December 2006)

O'Donnell, Bill, telephone interview (29 April 2006)

Pearson, Noel, personal interview (19 October 2005)

Sheridan, Jim, personal interview (10 May 2007)

Sheridan, Peter, personal interview (27 September 2005)

Stein, Sol, personal interview (20 September 2005)

NON-PRINT SOURCES

RADIO

Christy Brown: A Celebration, by Libby Purves, prod. John Skrine (BBC Radio 4, 25 December 1981)

TELEVISION

The Story of Christy Brown, dir. Joe Dunn (Radharc Films, Radio Telefís Éireann, 1962)

FILM

My Left Foot, dir. Jim Sheridan, starring Cyril Cusack, Daniel Day-Lewis, Adrian Dunbar, Brenda Fricker, Ray McAnally, Ruth McCabe, Hugh O'Connor, Fiona Shaw (Granada, 1989)

PRINT SOURCES

Auden, W.H., *Collected Poems* (Faber & Faber, London, 1966)

Barton, Ruth, *Jim Sheridan: Framing the Nation* (Liffey Press, Dublin, 2002)

Beckett, Samuel, *Molloy, Malone Dies, The Unnamable* (John Calder, London, 1994)

Behan, Brendan, *Borstal Boy* (Hutchinson, London, 1958)

Behan, Brendan, and Aubrey Dillon-Malone, *The Brothers Behan* (Ashfield Press, Dublin, 1998)

Brown, Christy, *A Shadow on Summer* (Secker & Warburg, London, 1974)

Brown, Christy, *A Promising Career* (Secker & Warburg, London, 1982)

Brown, Christy, *Background Music* (Secker & Warburg, London, 1973)

Brown, Christy, *Collected Poems* (Mandarin and Minerva, London, 1982)

Brown, Christy, *Come Softly to My Wake* (Secker & Warburg, London, 1971)

Brown, Christy, *Down All the Days* (Secker & Warburg, London, 1970)

Brown, Christy, *My Left Foot* (Secker & Warburg, London, 1994)

Brown, Christy, *Of Snails and Skylarks* (Secker & Warburg, London, 1977)

Brown, Christy, *Wild Grow the Lilies* (Secker & Warburg, London, 1976)

Collins, Pan, *It Started on The Late Late Show* (Ward River Press, Dublin, 1981)

Collis, John Stewart, *The Worm Forgives the Plough* (Barrie and Jenkins, London, 1988)

Collis, Robert, *To Be a Pilgrim: The Autobiography of Robert Collis* (Secker & Warburg, London, 1975)

Collis, Robert, *Marrowbone Lane* (Runa Press, Dublin, 1943)

Connaughton, Shane, and Jim Sheridan, *My Left Foot* (Faber & Faber, London, 1989)

Cronin, Anthony, *Dead as Doornails* (Poolbeg Press, Dublin, 1980)

Davies, Hunter, *Hunting People* (Mainstream Publishing, Edinburgh, 1994)

Davis, Lennard J., *Enforcing Normalcy* (Verso, New York, 1995)

Davis, Lennard J. (ed.), *The Disability Studies Reader* (Routledge, London, 1997)

Dolan, Terence, *A Dictionary of Hiberno-English* (Gill & Macmillan, Dublin, 1998)

Jenkins, Garry, *Daniel Day-Lewis: The Fire Within* (Sidgwick & Jackson, London, 1994)

Kearns, Kevin C., *Dublin Tenement Life: An Oral History* (Gill & Macmillan, Dublin, 1994)

Kiberd, Declan, *Irish Classics* (Granta, London, 2000)

Kiberd, Declan, *The Irish Writer and the World* (Cambridge University Press, 2005)

Liddy, James, *The Doctor's House* (Salmon Publishing, Cliffs of Moher, Co. Clare, 2004)

Liddy, James, *On the Raft with Fr. Roseliep* (Arlen House, Galway, 2006)

MacKillop, James (ed.), *Irish Cinema from* The Quiet Man *to* Dancing at Lughnasa (Syracuse University Press, New York, 1999)

McCormack, John, *The Story of Dublin* (Mentor Books, Dublin, 2000)

McGahern, John, *The Barracks* (Faber & Faber, London, 2000)

O'Connor, Ulick, *A Cavalier Irishman: The Ulick O'Connor Diaries 1970–1981* (John Murray, London, 2001)

Pierce, David (ed.), *Irish Writing in the Twentieth Century: A Reader* (Cork University Press, 2000)

Quinn, Antoinette, *Patrick Kavanagh: A Biography* (Gill & Macmillan, Dublin, 2001)

Roseliep, Raymond, *Love Makes the Air Light* (Norton, New York, 1965)

Wolfe, Thomas, *Look Homeward, Angel* (Charles Scribner, New York, 1957)

JOURNALS

Arena, No. 1, Spring 1963
Arena, No. 3, Summer 1964
The Holy Door, No. 1, Summer 1965
The Holy Door, No. 3, Spring 1966
Poetry Ireland, No. 2, Spring 1963

INDEX

Abbey Theatre 43, 88, 106, 110, 114, 166, 185
abortion debate 213
Agnew Somerville Gallery 157, 204
Arena 112, 118
Argos 108
Aristotle 5
Arts Council 185
Auden, W.H. 6, 222–3
Augustine, St 127
'Autumnal' 111

Background Music 177
Banville, John 144–7, 148, 149, 150
Barry, Kevin 100, 193
BBC 80, 88, 90, 108, 133, 151, 159
Beaverbrook, Lord 144
Beckett, Samuel 90, 191, 194
Behan, Brendan 11–12, 60–1, 105–6, 112–14, 130, 131, 133, 134, 174, 175, 182, 185, 191, 193, 195, 217, 218
Behan, Dominic 130
Behan, Kathleen 130
Belfrage, Julian 205
Benson, Sheila 211
Bernard (fellow patient of Dr Collis) 73
Bewley, Victor 42, 45
Bible, the 87
Blythe, Ernest 88

Booker Prize 145
Born on the Fourth of July 213
Bradbury, Malcolm 145
Brando, Marlon 198
Bray, Barbara 90
'Brendan' 119
Brendan Behan's Island 112
Brien, Alan 173–4
Brompton Chest Hospital 76
Brooke, Rupert 87
Brown, Ann (Jones; sister) 19, 23, 31, 74, 79, 113, 116, 138, 139, 165, 169, 180: husband Willy 117, 139, 165, 172–3; care for Christy after death of mother 139, 167; sharing house with Christy 165; and Christy's anger 172–3; on Christy on television 176; fears for Christy 180; and Christy's death 190; and film of *My Left Foot* 205–6, 207
Brown, Bridget (mother): death of 17–18, 138–9; birth and early life 18–19; children surviving beyond infancy 19; marriage 19; senses something different about Christy 21; determined that Christy should not be put in home 23; told Christy was 'mental defective' 23–4; wants normal life for Christy 24; closeness to Christy 26;

reads and sings with Christy 27, 32; teaches Christy to read and write 28, 29, 32, 33–4, 35; religiousness 33; worries over Christy's future 33; buys wheelchair for Christy 39; last child and illness following birth 42; and Katriona Maguire 44; Lourdes trip and 55, 56; builds a room for Christy 61–3; and helping Christy's writing 74; at launch party for *My Left Foot* 78; and death of husband 82–3; job with Dublin Corporation 84; heart attack and burst ulcer 95; and Brendan Behan 113; health deteriorating 130; death 138–9

Brown, Christy: birth 11, 20; symptoms of cerebral palsy 11, 15, 21, 22–3; income from writing 14, 84, 90, 124, 157; novels 14, 90, 127, 134, 139, 170, 176, 180, 190–1; poetry 14, 90, 111–12, 170, 177, 180, 189, 192; position in family 14–15; letters of 16, 215–16; and mother's death 17, 138–9; partial suffocation at birth 20, 23; diagnosis 21; and doctors 23, 26, 36–7, 45, 181; chariot (go-cart) 24–5, 37–8; developing language skills 25; muscle spasms 25; speech therapy 25, 72, 73–4, 79, 86; eating difficulties 26, 36, 189–90; mobility of big toe on left foot 27; picks up chalk with toes 27–8; learning to read and write 28, 29, 32, 33–4, 35, 37; poem for mother 28–9, 168; loneliness of 31; bird images 32; isolation of 32; style of communication 34–5;

lack of formal education 34, 70; anger 35, 172–3, 208; voice as writer 35; importance of left foot 36; importance of reading and writing 36, 38; initial understanding of his difference 38–9, 40; writing and disability 38–9; and depression 39, 49, 54–5, 121, 136–7, 138, 139–40; hatred of appearance 39, 109; and human condition of loneliness 39; and Katriona Maguire 41, 42, 45, 46, 47–9; painting 47, 115, 134–5, 157, 159; wins painting competition 47–8; sexuality 49–50; plays 50–1, 89, 114; rebelliousness 50; adolescence 51–2; and classical music 54, 121; trip to Lourdes 55–7; and Dickens 58, 71; first accurate diagnosis 60; physiotherapy for 61,65, 66–7, 70; a room built for 61–3; writing style 71; speech difficulties and therapy 25, 72–4, 75, 79, 86, 96, 109, 117, 207; interest in geometry 75; and fund-raising 76; interviews with 78–80, 153–5, 155–6 171–6; typewriters 78, 108, 158; radio programme about 80; and Beth Moore 81, 82, 85–6, 90, 91, 93–102, 108, 121, 124–6, 127, 130, 140–1, 155–6, 165–6, 176, 221; first real love affair 81; life change 81; need for love 81–2; death of father 82–3; romanticism 81–2, 94, 101, 164; abandons medical treatment 85; absorption of books 86–7; gramophone 86; reading works aloud 86; 'Totem Pole' 86; desire to write a play 87–8,

89, 115; grows beard 87; and Disabled Artists Association 88–9, 90, 95, 108, 115, 127–9, 133; passion for theatre 88, 115; drinking 91, 101, 103, 104, 105, 117–18, 133, 138, 139, 141, 155, 173, 180, 190; exhaustion 91, 95; letters to Beth Moore lost 94; trips to America 90, 95–101, 121, 124–6, 127, 153–6; new-found physical independence 98–9; obnoxiousness of 104; desire to produce lasting art 105, 106–7; buys car 108; ear for language 109; and rewriting 109–10; RTÉ documentary about 109; 'Sunlight and Snow' 111; 'Frostbite' 112; drinking and speech 117; help using toilet 118–19, 184; income from painting 127; money problems 129–30; adoration of mother 130; on Irish literary scene 131; and Patrick Kavanagh 131–3; fervour for living 133; on difficulty of living 136–8; first collection of poetry 139; on deprivation 140; liking for shocking people 151; new wheelchair 157; first meeting with Mary Carr 163, 164; and Mary Carr 163–7, 168–70, 172, 177, 187–8, 189–90; holiday in south of Ireland 167; wedding to Mary 169–70; and media 170–6; comparisons with other writers 175; leaves Dublin 177–8; loses contact with family and friends 178, 187, 188; 'drying out' 181; and Peter Sheridan 182–7; death 189–90; funeral 193; obituaries 194–5; plaque put up for 221;

see also under names of works
Brown, Danny (brother) 19, 42
Brown, Eamonn (brother) 14, 19, 37, 62, 108, 169: and writing My Left Foot 70–1, 74
Brown, Francis (brother) 19, 74, 75, 104, 169, 208
Brown, Jim (brother) 19, 33, 169, 170
Brown, Lizzie ('Titch'; sister) 19, 33
Brown, Mary (wife): Christy meets 163; relationship with Christy 163–7; alcoholism 164, 190; first husband 164; relationship with Christy develops 165–7, 168–70; difficulties of marriage to Christy 167; affairs 169, 176; absences in London 176, 179; and Christy's death 189–90; Christy's funeral 193
Brown, Mona (Byrne; sister) 19, 21–2, 25, 27, 33, 67, 117, 119, 138, 169, 209–10
Brown, Paddy (brother) 19, 20, 21, 24–5, 27, 37, 47, 169
Brown, Patrick (father) 19, 45, 62, 77, 209: work as bricklayer 20, 26; care for Christy 26, 209–10; and Lourdes trip 56; and room for Christy 62–3; death 82–3; burial 83–4; roughness 158
Brown, Peter (brother) 19, 33, 38
Brown, Seán (brother) 19, 54, 75, 80–1, 211: Christy's letters to 18, 31, 124, 125, 135–6, 139–40, 143–4, 166, 169, 177, 178; on Mary Brown (wife) 163
Brown, Tony (brother) 19, 33, 95, 104
Bull Alley Street: National Association for Cerebral Palsy 67, 72, 73

Byrne, Gay 175–6, 182
Byrne, Tom (brother-in-law) 117–18

Cahill, Martin 'The General' 14
Cannes Film Festival 210, 211
Carr, Mary *see* Brown, Mary (wife)
Carroll, Mr (DAA art teacher) 89, 95
cerebral palsy: Christy Brown born with 11, 15; athetoid 15, 22; ignorance about 22, 67; meaning of the words 22; symptoms 22
cerebral palsy clinic, Dublin 66–7, 70, 72, 76, 105, 202
Cerebral Palsy Ireland 67 *see also* National Association for Cerebral Palsy
Channel 4 207
Collins, Pan 176
Collis, Eirene 59, 63–5, 67, 70
Collis, Maurice 71
Collis, Dr Robert 23: and Katriona Maguire 42, 43–4; autobiographies 43, 58, 71, 78, 114; *The Silver Fleece* 43, 71, 114; first meets Christy Brown 45; and Christy as artist 53; career 58–61; *To Be a Pilgrim* 58, 78; and treatment centre for cerebral palsy 58, 67; diagnosis of Christy 60; examines Christy 65; cerebral palsy clinic 66; *The Barrel Organ* 71; *Marrowbone Lane* 71; plays written by 71; and *My Left Foot* 72, 75–6, 77, 116, 203, 207; teaching Christy about writing 72, 74, 109; fund-raising 76; in Germany 76; and publication of Christy's work 76, 77–8; acting as Christy's accountant 80–1, 85; and Christy's trip to

America 97, 100; literary work with Christy 107–8, 143; and Brendan Behan 60–1, 114; death 179
Collis, Robert 23
Come Softly to My Wake 139
'Come Softly to My Wake' 192
Connaughton, Shane 18, 136, 199, 200–1, 202, 203, 204, 212, 214
Cork 167
Cronin, Anthony 133
Cruise, Tom 213

David Frost Show, The 154–5
Davies, Aubrey 148
Davies, Hunter 164, 166, 167, 171–2, 173
Day, Patricia 152–3
Day-Lewis, Cecil 71, 78, 86
Day-Lewis, Daniel: awards for *My Left Foot* 13, 18, 207, 211, 212, 213; playing Christy 136, 201–2, 203, 204–5, 205–6, 208, 209, 210, 211, 217
Degas, Edgar 135
Delahunt, Katriona *see* Maguire, Katriona
Detroit News 153
Devlin, Alan 199–200
Dickens, Charles 58, 71, 81, 86
Disabled Artists Association (DAA) 88–9, 90, 95, 108, 115, 127–9, 133
Dolmen Press 11, 108
Down All the Days 14, 49, 114, 125, 144, 162, 167: quoted from 64, 150–1; 'Red Magso' in 134–5; stage adaptation 136, 182, 183, 185–7, 194; completed 139; admiration of 144–5, 148–9; launch party for 146–7; reviews 147–8, 152; translation rights 148; Christy's excitement over 149;

nature of 149–51; shocking
nature of 149–50; prose style
150; success of 151, 152; US
publication 152–3; and Beth
Moore 155; and Peter Sheridan
182, 183; rights to 200–1
Dublin: tenements 18, 19–20,
43, 44; housing 19–20, 43,
44; health conditions 42–3,
59; University College 42,
222; Project Arts Centre 183;
Christy Brown and 218–19;
National Archives 222; *see also*
following entries
Dublin Corporation 62, 84
Dublin Tourist Board 221
Dubliners, The 159, 199
Dunbar, Adrian 50–1, 208, 216,
218–19

Easter Rising 19, 83
'Echo' 118
Edwards, Hilton 43, 71
Ekland, Britt 25
Enable Ireland 67 *see also* National
Association for Cerebral Palsy
'End' 192
Epstein, Patricia 26–7
Evening Herald 46, 191
Evening Press 85, 104–5

Farrer, David 139, 143, 144–7,
148–9, 152–3, 177, 198
Feehan, Captain Seán 88–9, 115–
16, 128
Fitzgerald, F. Scott 31
Flack, Roberta 155
'For My Mother' 28–9, 168
Forster, Margaret 171: letter from
Christy 161–2
Four Roads, the 124
French, Percy 218
Fricker, Brenda 203, 206–7: Oscar
win 18

Friel, Brian 132, 215
Frost, David 154–5
'Frostbite' 112

Gate Theatre 43
Glasnevin Cemetery 193
go-carts 24
Good Housekeeping 78, 81
Granada Films 211, 212
Grant, Roger 167
Greene, Graham 31
Greenwood, Walter 43–4
Gresham Hotel 76
Guthrie, Mr (teacher) 74–5

Harcourt Street Children's Hospital
26, 67
Harris, Richard 78, 159–60, 169,
201
Hartnett, Michael 118, 132
Hawthorne, Nathaniel 100
Hepburn, Katharine 100
Hickey, Tom 202
Holy Door, The 118, 119
Hostelry, The 90
Hotel, The 107, 109, 114, 203–4
Houseman & Son Foundation 96
Hurt, John 205
Huston, John 76

IBM 108, 158
'In Retrospect' 111
Inmates 197
Inside I'm Dancing 214
'Invitation to the Trance' 80
Ireland America Society 76
Irish Independent 194
Irish language 216–17
Irish Republican Brotherhood 19
Irish Times 26, 119, 147, 194, 195
Ives, Burl 76

J.A. Miller & Son 78, 108
Jenny (childhood friend) 49

Jesus Christ 134
John Bull 78
Joyce, James 12, 106, 147, 152, 164, 172, 194, 195, 217

Kael, Pauline 208–9
Kavanagh, Patrick 131–3, 134, 221
Keane, John B. 105, 106
Kearns, Kevin C. 42
Kennelly, Brendan 132, 177, 194–5
Kerry 164, 177–8, 179, 182, 183, 187, 188, 190
Kiberd, Professor Declan 15, 217
Kierkegaard, Søren 222
Kimmage: 14, 20, 37, 97, 113, 158, 161, 221–2
'Kind of Lament for Patrick Kavanagh', 'A' 132–3
Kline, Kevin 18
Kovic, Ron 213

Late Late Show, The 175–6, 182
Laverty, Maura 86
Leonore (DAA agent) 89
Lewis, Jerry Lee 184, 195
Liddy, James 90, 108, 111–12, 118, 132
Life 147, 152
Lisheen 165, 166, 168, 169, 170, 176, 177
Longford, Lord 71, 78
'Lost Prize', 'The' 112
Lourdes 55–7, 66, 193
Lynch, Brian 118–19, 132, 216

McAnally, Ray 106, 110, 111, 114–15, 202, 203–4
McAuley, James J. 111
McCabe, Eugene 131–2
McClory, Kevin 159, 170, 198
McColgan, John 201
McGahern, John 115
McGuinness, Frank 150, 151, 214–16

Mac Liammóir, Micheál 43, 71
Mab Cottage 178, 182, 183, 184, 185
Maguire, Katriona: letters from Christy 41, 48, 53, 65, 69–70, 99, 103, 109, 128–9, 131–2, 135, 178, 221; love for Christy 41, 46; and Dr Collis 42, 43–4, 74; as Lady Almoner 42; meets Christy Brown 42; altruistic ideals 44; and Bridget Brown 44; and Brown family 45, 46; forms bond with Christy 45, 46; teaching Christy 45; understanding Christy 45, 49; and Christy's depressions 49; and Christy's Lourdes trip 55, 193; at *My Left Foot* launch party 78; and Christy's writing 127; reaction to Christy's engagement 168; at premiere of *Down All the Days* 187; and Christy's death 193–4; and film of *My Left Foot* 203, 207
Mahon, Brid 23
Mahon, Maura 104
Marrowbone Lane 43–4, 71
Marrowbone Lane Fund 42, 43, 45, 58, 67, 76, 95, 193
Martin (friend of Christy) 117
May, Freddie 116–17
Mercier Press 88, 116
Middlesex Hospital 63
Miller, J.A. 78
Miller, Liam 11, 108
Miramax Films 210
'Modern Idyll' 119
Mooney, Ria 87–8
Moore, Beth 81, 82, 85–6, 91, 94–5, 96, 99, 124–7: meeting with Christy 90, 97–8; letters to 93–4; marriage 94; European tours 121, 165; dislike of being in background 155–6; Christy curtails visit to 156; Christy

ends relationship with 165–6;
and *Down All the Days* 165;
and *A Shadow on Summer*
176–7
Moore, Brian 131
Moore, Deac 81, 97, 121, 165
Moving Out 113
Mrs Brennan 107, 215
Muldoney, Paul 104–5
Mullane, Father 74
Murray, James 80
My Left Foot (book): on learning
to write 32, 34; and otherness
38–9; on understanding of his
difference 38–9; on Jenny 49;
on music 54; on Lourdes trip
57; progress of 69–70, 74, 75;
beginning of 70; second draft
72, 74; on speech therapy 73;
chapter read at fund-raising
event 76–7; publication 76,
77; launch party for 78;
success of 78; translations 78;
income from 84, 89, 108; radio
adaptation 88; sequel to 90;
paperback edition 116, 128;
Christy embarrassed by 133,
183; original copy of 222
My Left Foot (film) 50, 195, 198–
210, 217: Oscar nominations
18, 213; screenplay for
136; rights to 198, 200–1;
controversy and 207, 213;
at Cannes Film Festival 210;
reviews 211; awards nominated
for 214; *see also under* Day-
Lewis, Daniel

National Association for Cerebral
Palsy 67, 72
National Library of Ireland 72, 202
New York Times 173, 211
1916 Rising 19, 83
Noonan, Gillman 190–1

O'Brien, Edna 131
O'Casey, Seán 105–6, 112, 182,
183, 195
O'Connor, Carroll 198
O'Connor, Frank 43, 71
O'Connor, Hugh 209
O'Connor, Jack 188
O'Connor, Ulick 157: on Behan
60–1; on Christy Brown 67,
176, 179; meeting with Christy
116; on Ann Jones 139; diaries
176, 179; on *My Left Foot* 204
O'Donnell, Bill 167–8, 181–2, 192,
193, 197
Observer Magazine 164, 171
Of Snails and Skylarks 189
O'Faoláin, Seán 71, 72, 86, 108
Old Theatre Royal, Dublin 84
Olivier, Laurence 205, 209
Open University 34
Oscar Theatre, Dublin 185

Parbrook, Somerset 187–8
Parkinson 159–60
Pearson, Noel: Oscar nomination
18; on Christy's fearlessness
133; first meets Christy 157–9;
and Christy's marriage to Mary
169–70; on Thomas Wolfe 175;
on Christy and suicide 178;
Christy loses touch with 187;
and Christy's death 192; and
Down All the Days 198, 200,
216; and *My Left Foot* 199,
201–2, 203, 209, 210, 211,
212, 214
Phelps, Dr (Johns Hopkins
Hospital) 59
Picasso, Pablo 126
Pike Theatre 114
Poetry Ireland 108–9, 111–12
Promising Career, A 190–1, 195,
197

Radharc 109, 206
Rathcoole 165, 166, 168, 179, 190
  see also Lisheen
'Red Magso' 134–5
Richard III 205, 209
Rodgers, W.R. 88
Rolling Stone 211
Roseliep, Raymond 90, 126–7
Rosencrantz and Guildenstern Are Dead 125
Rotunda Hospital 20, 42, 59, 67
Royal Dublin Society 86
RTÉ 109, 133, 151, 192, 206
Russell, Bertrand 75

St Brendan's Hospital 73
St Kevin's Hospital, Dublin 95
St Patrick's Mission Society,
  Wicklow 80
'Sally' 85–6
Sands, Bobby 185
Schiele, Egon 50
Secker & Warburg 77, 78, 139,
  145, 148–9, 156, 177, 190, 197
Sellers, Peter 25
Shadow on Summer, A 176–7
Shakespeare, William 87
Share, Bernard 147–8
Shaw, Fiona 203, 207, 208
Shaw, George Bernard 87, 160
Sheehan, Bobby 87, 119
Sheehan, Dr Patricia 72–3, 85, 86–
  7, 89, 90, 95, 100, 101, 105,
  119–21, 169, 177, 178, 187,
  188, 202–3, 207
Sheridan, Jim 78, 182, 183, 185–6,
  194, 199–200 214, 216: Oscar
  nominations 18; and *My Left
  Foot* 185, 186, 200–1, 204,
  212
Sheridan, Peter 78, 182–7, 186,
  195, 216
Simon & Schuster 77
Simpson, Alan 114

Smith, Gus 185
Solomons, Bethel 59
Stamford Advocate 125, 156–7
Stegmann, Arnulf Erich 88–9,
  128–9
Stein, Sol 152–4, 161, 174
Stewart, John 71
Still, Sir Frederick 59
Stone Boat, the 113, 117, 118, 119,
  124, 206, 209
Stone, Oliver 213
Stoppard, Tom 125
Sunday Independent 47, 177, 185
Sunday Press 23, 24
Sunday Times 162, 171–2
'Sunlight and Snow' 111
'Surf' 118

tenements, Dublin 18, 19–20, 43,
  44
'Terminal Thoughts' 189
Today 153–4
'Totem Pole' 86
Twain, Mark 100

United Cerebral Palsy Association
  96, 99
United Nations 100

Waldorf-Astoria Hotel 99
Warnants, Dr Louis 53, 61, 63, 64,
  66
Weber, Richard 111
Weinstein, Harvey 210, 212
Welles, Orson 205
'W.H. Auden' 222–3
Wild Grow the Lilies 180
Williams, Tennessee 50, 216
Wolfe, Thomas 175, 200
Wulf, Peter Liman 125

Yeats, W.B. 75, 100, 152, 160, 221